MEMOIR

UPON THE

LIGHT-HOUSE ILLUMINATION

OF THE

COASTS OF FRANCE.

BY

LÉONCE REYNAUD,

INSPECTOR GENERAL OF BRIDGES AND ROADS, DIRECTOR OF THE LIGHTING AND BUOY SERVICE, &c.

TRANSLATED FOR THE LIGHT-HOUSE BOARD OF THE UNITED STATES

BY

Rear Admiral THORNTON A. JENKINS, U. S. N.,

NAVAL SECRETARY.

WASHINGTON:

GOVERNMENT PRINTING OFFICE.

1871.

INTRODUCTION.

This Memoir has been prepared by order of His Excellency the Minister of Agriculture, Commerce, and Public Works, and as I do not desire that more credit may be given to me for the publication than that which properly belongs to me, I deem it to be my duty to recall to the attention of the reader the fact that the Lens system for light-house illumination was invented by Augustin Fresnel; that the actual organization of the Light-house Service is due, fundamentally, to the worthy brother of that illustrious savant, Léonor Fresnel; and that the judicious plan of distribution of our seacoast illumination has been successfully worked out by the Commission of Lighting, (*Commission des Phares.*)

The task which devolved upon me, when I had the honor to be called to the direction of the Light-house, &c., Service, has been lightened by the hearty co-operation of others. The Engineers of the maritime Departments have directed, with their habitual devotion, and with entire success, the works confided to them, which were sometimes attended with danger, and often very difficult of execution; and my associates of the Central Service (the Engineers, Messrs. Degrand and Allard) have most usefully co-operated with me in studying new dispositions to be made of apparatus, and also in the numerous experiments which will be found recorded in this work.

I must not omit to add, that the Administration of Public Works, appreciating fully the great importance and usefulness of the aids to navigation on our coasts, in the double aspect, of the general interests of humanity, and of the development of the naval and commercial greatness of the nation, has always accorded its approbation to the recommendations of the Commission of Lights; its encouragement in the prosecution of experimental researches and promising innovations; and its assistance in carrying out the great undertaking embraced in the original plan of illumination, which is now nearly completed.

(Signed) L. REYNAUD.

NOVEMBER, 1864.

MEMOIR

UPON

THE LIGHTING AND BEACONAGE

OF THE

COASTS OF FRANCE.

PART I.—ILLUMINATION.

CHAPTER I.

GENERAL DISPOSITIONS.

I. DISTRIBUTION OF LIGHTS.

The entrances to ports and the mouths of navigable streams were for a long time regarded as the only places at which it was needful to establish lights for the benefit of the mariner, and the chief object and effort then was to give as great a range as possible to the lights thus placed to mark those points. It is now, and has been for some time, quite different; the requirements of navigation having become so much greater, it follows, as a necessary consequence, that they should be more amply and fully met, and, in being more fully developed, the illumination of maritime coasts rests upon very different laws from what it formerly did, as it is now recognized that the greater number of the localities hitherto considered of primary importance need only be provided with lights of a secondary character, while the primary lights are assigned to positions where they will render better service to the mariner.

As it is near the line of the seacoast that the most formidable and serious obstacles to navigation exist, it is, as a natural consequence, the coast line, above all, which should be first pointed out to the approaching vessel. The line of the seacoast presents a series of capes, (headlands and deep indentations,) variously marked, which may be considered as the salient angles of a polygon, circumscribing all outlying rocks and reefs, and a light is now placed to mark each of these, so that the mariner is warned of danger at as great a distance from the land as the elevation of the light and the power of the illuminating apparatus will allow. The distances between the positions of these primary seacoast lights are so arranged with reference to their respective range that it is now impossible for any vessel to approach the coast within a reasonable distance during clear weather without seeing at least one light to warn the master of danger.

These lights, which have been established, essentially and primarily, to mark the approach to the coast line, are designated as SEACOAST or LAND-FALL LIGHTS. They are of the first order and class, and have the greatest power and range.

After having warned the mariner by these outlying lights, placed on the most salient points of the seacoast, of his proximate distance from the coast line and dangers, and given him a first instruction as to the course he should steer, it then becomes necessary that he should be provided with the means for safely steering to the place to which he is bound, and for that purpose recourse is had to lights of less power and range. In the sea space or indentation, of greater or less extent, and more or less open, embraced between two first-order seacoast lights, there are points, or secondary capes, islands, rocks, reefs, and sandbanks, the positions of which it is the interest of the navigator to know; there are channels also whose direction it is both necessary and useful to mark for his safety, and these places are now marked by lights whose powers and ranges are regulated by the distances at which it is needful for them to be seen. These lights differ from those of the first order not only in intensity, but some of them illuminate only a small arc of the horizon, others larger arcs, and others again the entire horizon, according to circumstances.

Finally, the course for the vessel being thus carefully marked out, to near the port or anchorage which is to end the voyage, it suffices to place a small light on one or each of the banks, piers, or breakwaters, to point out the entrance. Many of these small lights belonging to tidal harbors are not exhibited until the tide has reached a certain determined height. The greater number of the harbors of this description are lighted by two lights, one employed as a *tide light*, and exhibited only at certain heights of the tide, while the other is kept as a permanent light, to mark the locality and position at all times.

During foggy or thick weather, when the ranges of the first order seacoast lights are greatly diminished in power and extent, the secondary lights come in and fill up the gaps in the primary illumination, and thus maintain its continuity, or at least diminish in a great degree the extent of those portions of the coast which are not lighted.

The range (or distance at which they may be seen) assigned to first order lights varies from 18 to 27 nautical miles,* according to their

* 1 nautical mile of 60 to the degree = 1,852 meters = 2,025.4 yards, in round numbers.
1 meter = 39.371 inches = 1.094 yards.
1 kilometer = 39,371.0 inches = 1,093.6389 yards.

character. The other orders and classes of lights, being more diverse in character, have ranges varying from two to twenty miles. These latter lights are divided into three orders, according to the quantity of light emanating from the focus of the apparatus.

Lights so greatly multiplied would expose the mariner to the risk of making fatal mistakes, were it not that ample means have been devised for varying their characteristic distinctions in such a way as to render it easy to provide distinctions so that one may not be mistaken for another. Those means were not available when the light was necessarily produced by the combustion of wood or of coal; at least only to the extent of grouping several lights at or about the same point or locality, which would be extremely limited in practical utility, and would besides be attended with great annual expense. But the invention and introduction of parabolic reflectors with double current of air (Argand) lamps, and the still later and much more valuable inventions of Augustin Fresnel, allow the characteristic distinctions to be varied as far as may be necessary or desirable, and increase enormously in proportion, at the same time, the powers and ranges of the lights.

It is of the greatest importance that the lights of the first order, and those which, on some particular points, fulfil the necessary requirements of great seacoast or "land-fall" lights, should be very marked in their characteristic distinctions, so that the mariner may be duly and unmistakably apprised of his true position, and enabled to rectify any errors of his "reckoning" before he shall have approached the coast too near for safety, under all circumstances of weather. But it is not necessary that each light should have a particular or special characteristic distinction. It will be quite sufficient that the distances between those of the same characteristic distinction, on the same and adjacent coast, exceed any error of position which might result under ordinary circumstances of weather and navigation. To fix a limit to that error is doubtless by no means easy; nevertheless, the "Commission des Phares" determined that a navigator should not be more than 80 miles in error of his true position, (out of his reckoning,) except in rare and extraordinary cases, and under such circumstances of weather and want of opportunity for accurate observations for latitude and time, he should be extremely cautious in approaching the land at night. Warned, however, of his approach to the land by seeing a light, if in doubt as to his position and the light seen, he should keep well off the land during the night, and until he satisfies himself of his position.

It may be remarked, however, that a mistake which might be easily made when but one light is in sight, would not prevent its instant recognition when several lights are visible at the same time, of different characteristic distinctions, numbers, and relative positions. Under such circumstances, shorter distances may sometimes be allowed than those already spoken of. For example, the first order fixed lights of the Isle of Groix and the Isle of Yeu are only distant 72 miles from each other; but the first one cannot be seen on the same bearing as the second, without seeing at the same time either the fixed light varied by flashes on the Isle of Penfret, or the eclipse (revolving) light showing a bright flash once in every minute on Belle-Isle-en-Mer, which will prevent the possibility of error on the part of the navigator.

Analogous considerations allow the use of the same characteristic distinctions for the light at Carteret, and the one on Cape Fréhel, although they are only forty-six miles apart.

It is thus seen that the general principles upon which the illumination of the coasts of France are based may be summed up as follows:

The approaches to the salient points of the coast line are marked by lights of the greatest power and range, sufficiently diversified by different characteristic distinctions to properly define their respective positions, and placed in such proximity to each other as to prevent the navigator from getting within the limit of outlying dangers during clear weather, before seeing at least one seacoast light to warn him of his approach to the land; and then the in-shore illumination, by lights varied in appearance, and the ranges regulated by the distances at which it is necessary to see them in guiding safely into port.

These principles were set forth and adopted for the first time in the report and programme presented to the "Commission des Phares," by Admiral Rossel, and approved September 9, 1825. They have never been lost sight of, but it may be readily understood that it has not always been possible to apply them rigorously. A coast line of such great extent, and so broken and varied in its character, would not allow of any absolute plan being unexceptionally carried out. Thus, externally to the sides of the ideal polygon, of which the lights of the first class and order occupy the summits, an islet, the head of a rock, or a sand bank may exist, which it may be necessary to mark, and a light secondary in character may suffice to meet the requirements of the navigator. Thus, on our Channel coast, for example, the group of the Seven Isles is situated to seaward of the line which connects the first order lights at the Heaux de Bréhat and the Isle de Bas, and upon which a light of the third order is placed. A similar arrangement obtains at the Isle Vierge, between the lights at the Isle de Bas and Ouessant.

Sometimes, too, the configuration of the coast line is such as not to permit the placing of two first order lights sufficiently near to each other for their arcs of illumination to cross, and in such cases the dark spaces left between the two first order lights are filled up by establishing a secondary light. A case of this kind will be seen by referring to the lights of La Héve and Barfleur, which are separated by a deep bay, and which latter is lighted by a third order light exhibited from the point of Ver; also to the lights of Belle-Isle and Isle of Yeu, between which the Pilier light is placed; to the lights of Agde and Faraman, the intervening space between which is lighted by the light at Aigues-Mortes.

It may also happen that a light which does not occupy the position of seacoast or "land-fall" light, should, however, have the power and range of a first-order light. The light of Fatouville, at the mouth of the river Seine, furnishes such an example and illustration, the object for which it was established and the configuration of the coast line at that point rendering it necessary to place it at such a distance inland that a less powerful intensity, and a tower of less height, would have produced a light of an insufficient range for the purposes of navigation.

And, lastly, when a cape whose position would seem to designate it as the proper place for the establishment of a first class light, but not being well marked or very prominent, and having points on either side of it which it is necessary to have lighted, such, for example, as the entrances to ports possessing a certain degree of importance, it will be well to leave it unmarked by a light, and erect the seacoast or "land-fall" light upon one or both of those minor points. For example, the Cape Antifer, which is situated between Fécamp and Havre, is not lighted, and the first order seacoast lights are placed on the heights which overlook the entrances to these ports. The low cape between Dunkerque and Gravelines, which has been treated in the same way, may be cited as another example.

For the remainder of the lights, it will suffice to examine the chart, where the positions will be seen, and their characteristic distinctions compared, to judge how far the general principles have been applied to them, and what were the geographical requirements and circumstances which sometimes intervened to prevent their being strictly conformed to.

II. CHARACTERISTIC DISTINCTIONS OF LIGHTS.

The programme agreed upon by the Light Commission, (*Commission des Phares*,) in 1825, approved of only three different kinds or characteristic distinctions of lights of the first order:

1. The fixed light;

2. The revolving light, with eclipses succeeding each other once in every minute, (1′ to 1″;) and,

3. The revolving light, with eclipses succeeding each other once in every half minute (30″ to 30″.)

A fixed light was always to be placed between two revolving or eclipse lights having different intervals of time between the flashes and eclipses. Lights of the same characteristic distinction would thus be separated as much as was considered to be necessary; but experience has shown that navigators of merchant vessels do not always pay sufficient attention to observing the differences of elapsed time between the flashes or eclipses of revolving lights which have been spoken of; besides, the number of lights has necessarily been so greatly increased beyond the anticipations of those who prepared the report and programme of 1825, that it was found necessary to introduce a much larger number of characteristic distinctions than was originally designed. One distinction, which may be said to belong to the infancy of the art, was adopted since the close of the last century for one of our most important seaports, that of Havre, and was continued exceptionally at this point by the programme of 1825. It consists of the exhibition of two first-order fixed lights side by side, at such a distance apart as to prevent their rays from blending into one beam, within the limit of their range of visibility, and so as always to be seen as belonging to one light station, or group.

This kind of characteristic distinction is, without doubt, objectionable, on account of the expense, which is nearly double that of a station with only one light, both for the original outlay for construction as well as for the annual maintenance and repair; but it has the merit of being very sharply and well defined, and is highly appreciated by navigators approaching that part of the coast. Many examples of this sort are found on the coasts of Great Britain. This distinction has been employed on the coast of France, within the last few years, in lighting the low, dangerous coast line in the vicinity of the mouth of the Canche, and also to that of the Gulf of Gascony, along the space comprised between the light of Cordouan and the basin of Arcachon.

Another distinctive characteristic, which was at first reserved for apparatus of the second and third orders, has since been applied to lights of the first order, viz., the fixed light varied by successive flashes and partial eclipses once in every three minutes, (3′ to 3′,) and of once in every four minutes, (4′ to 4′,) that is to say, having sufficiently long intervals between the brilliant flashes to prevent the lights from being mistaken for the ordinary revolving or eclipse lights. This distinction has been selected for the lights at Calais, Isle de Sein, Porquerolles, Sanguinaires and Porto-Vecchio, in order to avoid mistaking these lights for others in the same vicinity.

This may be reversed, to insure to an eclipse light another characteristic distinction, not less marked; that is to say, the rapidity with which the flashes succeed each other may be greatly increased.

The "Commission des Phares" has adopted recently, for a first-order light to be placed on a point of great importance, and one at which there should be no risk of confusion in the mind of the mariners in determining its true character and position, an apparatus whose eclipses will not be separated longer that for one and a half second, and thus produce a kind of scintillation. This is denominated a *scintillating light.* No fixed light will be seen between the intervals of the flashes.

Lastly, colored lights have been introduced to serve as characteristic distinctions. This mode of distinguishing lights was condemned at first in the most absolute manner; and they certainly present inconveniences which ought to prevent their use, except very rarely, and then only with great reserve. One serious objection to the use of color in distinguishing lights is, that the coloring matter reduces, in great proportion, the intensity of the light; and another is, that atmospheric conditions sometimes determine the color, which may lead to mistakes as to the real color of the light. But it is now known, and has been acknowledged, that these phenomena are not of so grave a character as had been previously attributed to them; and the "Commission des Phares," yielding to the solicitations of navigators, permitted at first the introduction of the red color as a means of distinguishing the lights of the smaller orders, and afterwards introduced it even for distinguishing lights of the first order. It also approved of the introduction of green as a distinction in some exceptional cases. The subject is one of too serious import not to have it seem necessary to make known the reasons upon which these decisions were based.

There are only three colors which are sufficiently marked and defined to be united with white as a means of distinguishing lights—red, green, and blue. They are produced by passing the rays of light emanating from the lamp-burner through properly-colored glass, and the photometric experiments made under ordinary circumstances, that is to say, at short distances, establish the fact that the tints sufficiently decided cause a loss of light which may reach even to 95 per cent. Red is, of all colors, that which is the most distinct for an equal amount of absorption of the luminous rays; and this is not its only comparative merit, considered in regard to maritime illumination, but it possesses another which is considerable, and has been proved by the experiments which will be reported and discussed when the question as to the disposition of apparatus arises. With equal intensity, the red light will be seen farther than the white light. If two lights, one red and the other white, appear to be of about equal intensity, as estimated according to the usual photometric means and processes, the flash or brilliancy of the red light will be carried beyond that of the white when they are both observed at great distances, and that effect will be still more marked as the distance from them is increased. The white light will cease to be visible before the red light. This phenomenon is above all very marked in certain states of the atmosphere, which will be readily understood, since fog generally has the effect of changing the color of white light to red,* from which it should be concluded that it offers less obstruction to the transmission of the red than to the other rays of light.

The observations which have been made at the light of Pontaillac, at the mouth of the Gironde, may be cited in illustration of this subject. This apparatus is arranged so as to exhibit a light which is alternately red and white, without any intervening eclipse between these appearances. Measured by the photometer, at about 8 meters† distance from the light, and at about 3 meters‡ distance from the instrument, the intensities were estimated to be 1,100 burners of the carcel lamp† for the white light, and about 700 burners for the red light. When near the light the white light appeared more brilliant than the red, but farther off it appeared to be equal, and still farther yet, the red was sometimes seen better than the white light. It has also been affirmed by some navigators that during foggy weather the red flashes have been seen before the white ones were visible. The distances at which these phenomena are produced vary with the state of the atmosphere.

It is seen, then, that the loss of light caused by coloring it red is not so great as had been previously supposed from experiments made upon lights at short distances, and, above all, that the red light becomes much less rapidly impaired during the existence of the most ordinary fogs than the white light, that is to say, under those circumstances which make it highly important to have brilliant lights.

The green and blue lights show, in this respect, the opposite of the red, as, indeed, might easily have been foreseen. They diminish in intensity much more rapidly in proportion than the white as the distance increases, and still more so as the atmosphere becomes thicker. This subject will be recurred to again.

It is a recognized fact that different states of the atmosphere cause lights to appear to be of different colors. It has been observed that during foggy weather white lights become of a reddish color or tinge, green approach in color or become white, and blue lights are not visible, or change to so pale a violet tint as to be mistaken for white. These phenomena ought assuredly to be gravely considered, but they lose much of their intrinsic importance when, instead of a single isolated light, there are two lights of different colors, and especially when one of them is red and the other white. If the white light should have a

* Some heavy fogs allow all the luminous rays to pass through them equally, and only have the effect of diminishing their intensity; they dim the lights without coloring them.

† 1 meter = 39.371 inches = 3 feet 3.371 inches.

‡ The carcel burner is the unity of the measure of light adopted in the lighting service, as will be seen further on in this work.

red tinge, then the red one becomes more intensely red; and thus both preserve their distinctive characters. The effect, however, would not be the same if the green were substituted for the red, they would still be distinguished, the one from the other, but instead of seeing white and green, they would appear to be red and white, without there being a very marked difference in color, and it would require an acuteness of sight which cannot be expected always to be found among observers to determine the true colors. The red color, therefore, appears to be superior from this point of view to any of the others.

Such were the considerations which caused the introduction of color as a characteristic distinction in light-house illumination, and the adoption of red almost exclusively for that purpose. They have equally determined the manner of using and the circumstances which will render the introduction of color advisable.

Red fixed lights have only been established at points where one or more fixed white lights are necessarily placed at the same time, in such a way as to render mistakes of color impossible. No colored fixed light of the first order has been established, as it is of primary importance that the over-sea voyager should not be led into error, or even have any hesitation in deciding as to the true characteristic of the first single light which he sees in approaching land.

Fixed lights of short range are often colored red for the sake of distinction, when it is feared those of the natural color might be mistaken for those on the streets, in dwellings, or on wharves, &c.

When piers or breakwaters of a port are distinguished by lights, one is habitually white and the other red.

The same rule applies equally to range lights, where it is necessary to diversify them; when their positions are such that the most distant may not always appear to the navigator above the other, one is always colored. Recourse is sometimes had to green, where there is danger of confusion from groups of lights in the vicinity.

Red is equally used for lights of the first order when they are not fixed. It is very evident that there can be no inconvenience in coloring lights by means of flashes varied in the manner already spoken of, when these flashes are not required to increase the power and range of the light, but merely to give the station a distinctive character. Instead of varying a fixed white light at intervals of three or four minutes by a period of much greater luminous intensity, it may be varied by changes to red. Color is substituted for the flash, and it always preserves its distinctive characteristic, for the reason that white immediately succeeds it.

A similar disposition has been made for revolving or eclipse lights. The flashes of these lights are colored, some red and others white;

sometimes they alternate, and sometimes a red flash is succeeded by two white flashes.

It will be seen, further on, that the apparatus is then arranged in such a way as to receive more of the luminous rays upon the colored panels than upon the others.

Finally, a new characteristic, based upon the intervention of two colors, has been recently adopted for a light of the third order which was not required to be seen at a great distance, and might lead to mistakes, if it had not been very decidedly and sharply distinguished from its immediate neighbors. This light is white, and becomes alternately red and green for some seconds, without there being intervening eclipses between the diverse luminous apparitions. When there is fog, the green flash will be reduced, in proportion more or less marked, and it may also become an eclipse at a certain distance; but navigators are not ignorant of the effects such a state of the atmosphere produces, and will always recognize the light as distinctively characterized. Some apparatus, similar as to their general disposition, only vary the white light by red flashes.

Thus, in the actual state of the lighting service of France, the first class seacoast lights have nine different distinctive characteristics:

WHITE LIGHTS.

1. Fixed light.
2. Eclipse light, once in every minute.
3. Eclipse light, once in every half minute.
4. Scintillating light.
5. Fixed light, varied by flashes.
6. Two fixed lights.

COLORED LIGHTS.

7. Fixed white light, varied by red flashes.
8. Eclipse light, with alternate red and white flashes.
9. Eclipse light, with two white flashes succeeded by a red flash.

It would be easy to obtain a greater number of characteristic distinctions by means of other combinations of the same elements, but, so far, there has been no necessity for them.

The same appearances, and others besides, such as the fixed red before referred to, the red eclipse light, and the alternate white and red with or without eclipses, the alternate white, red, white and green, are adapted to apparatus of the second and third orders.

As to lights of the fourth order, they are mostly fixed, and are distinguished by either position or color. They are not generally distinguished by eclipses, for the reason that the navigator is too near to the shore at the time when they are required to serve as his guides to allow of their ever being lost sight of. The arrangements which produce the different characters of lights will be pointed out when the subject of illuminating apparatus is reached.

III. RANGES OF THE LIGHTS.

The distance at which a light may be seen depends upon its intensity and upon its height above the level of the sea. There is, then, to be considered, the *luminous range* and the *geographical range.*

The considerations upon which these valuations are based will be examined in the order of succession.

LUMINOUS RANGES.

The power of illuminating apparatus is determined by means of photometric measurements, and the unity of measure adopted in experiments is the light of a carcel lamp, whose burner has a diameter of two hundredths of a meter, (0.02*m*.,) and consumes forty grammes (40) of colza oil per hour.

If the lights transmitted their rays or beams through a vacuum, the ranges would be in proportion to the square roots of the intensities, and it would be sufficient to know the distance at which a light of a known power may be seen by a person endowed with ordinary vision to determine the range of a light of a different intensity. Thus, in admitting that the light produced by a carcel lamp may be seen at the distance of 10 kilometers, it would be concluded that a fixed light of the first order, the intensity of which is equivalent to 630 carcel burners, ought to have a range of 251 kilometers*, and that the maximum brilliancy of the flash of an apparatus of the same order of eclipses once in every minute, which is equal to 5,075 carcel burners, should be 712 kilometers.*

But the atmosphere is not a transparent body; on the contrary, it is more or less opaque, which has the effect, concurrently with the distance, of weakening the luminous rays; and its action varies between extreme limits. There are some intensely dense fogs that arrest our most powerful lights at the distance of only a few meters. The ranges are then less than those which would be deduced from the law of which we have just spoken, and they depend upon the state of the atmosphere. It is evident, besides, that they also depend upon the clearness and acuteness of vision of, the observer. Elements so variable and difficult to accurately estimate, do not admit of our obtaining great accuracy of calculated results to express the ranges, nor of according to them much confidence, and yet there is inducement, even in a practical point of view, to study the question, and subject it to calculation.

---

* 1 kilometer = 39,371 inches = 1,093.6389 yards.

Let

L be the luminous intensity of an illuminating apparatus, or the quantity of light sent upon the unity of surface to the unity of distance, the quantity of light which comes from the carcel lamp already spoken of being taken for unity;

a the fraction of received light which can pass through a stratum of atmosphere whose thickness is equal to the unity of distance;

λ the smallest quantity of light, at the unity of distance, which the observer can see in an atmosphere whose transparency is complete;

x the range of the illuminating apparatus.

We should then have $\frac{L}{x^2} = \lambda$, if the transmission of light were through a vacuum, and $\frac{L a^x}{x^2} = \lambda$, if it were transmitted through the atmosphere.

It belongs to experiments to determine and make known the values to be given to the coefficients a and λ.

Bouguer has made observations upon the quantity of light which comes from a full moon at different elevations, to determine the diminution caused by a serene atmosphere, and the results found led him to assign to a the value of 0.973, the kilometer being the unity of distance.

A series of experiments have been undertaken by the engineers of the service, (Commission des Phares,) to determine the values which belong to that coefficient during a more or less foggy atmosphere, and to determine that which should be given to λ. They have consisted of observations, under diverse atmospheric circumstances, of lights of different intensities, and differently defined, and to measure the distances at which they ceased to be visible to an observer possessing ordinarily good sight. The illuminating apparatus was placed in front of the windows of the central lighting establishment, and the observations made from the Champ de Mars. They employed, in succession, different apparatus, and a lamp or candle, in front of which were placed a certain number of panes of glass, which absorbed a greater or less quantity of light, which had been previously ascertained.

Two observations, carefully made, sufficed to give the value of λ and that of a at the moment the experiments were made; consequently, in the relations

$$\frac{L' a^{x'}}{x'^2} = \lambda, \quad \frac{L'' a^{x''}}{x''^2} = \lambda,$$

we will know the quantities L′, L″, x' and x'', intensities and ranges, respectively, of the observed lights. But it is easy to see that experiments of that kind are not sufficiently precise to allow the dispensing with repetitions of them, and that confidence ought only to be given to the mean values thence deduced.

The table below shows the figures which have been assigned to L and found for x in the experiments which have been undertaken.

No. of order.	Date of the experiment.	Nature of the lighting apparatus.		Values of— L	Values of— x	Values of— $\log \frac{L}{x^2}$
				Burners.	*Kilom.*	
1	Oct. 24, 1860...	Candle of an intensity of 0.1 with—	13 panes	0.038	0.750	$\bar{2}.830$
			9 do.	0.050	0.830	$\bar{2}.861$
			5 do.	0.070	0.950	$\bar{2}.890$
			1 do.	0.094	1.010	$\bar{2}.964$
		Small lamp of an intensity of 0.32 with—	15 panes	0.106	1.030	$\bar{1}.000$
			12 do.	0.131	1.050	$\bar{1}.075$
			8 do.	0.176	1.130	$\bar{1}.139$
			4 do.	0.237	1.300	$\bar{1}.147$
2	Oct. 25, 1860...	Candle of an intensity of 0.13 with—	22 panes	0.026	0.965	$\bar{2}.446$
			7 do.	0.078	1.405	$\bar{2}.597$
3	Dec. 24, 1860...	Apparatus in striated glass, (seen below the optical axis)........		4.000	1.200	0.444
		Photophore, (seen below the optical axis)......................		40.000	1.600	1.194
4	Jan. 23, 1861, (from 8 to 9.)	Carcel lamp, unity..............		1.000	0.330	0.963
		Lamp of 3d order...............		4.400	0.380	1.484
		Lamp of 1st order, 23 burners, with 4 panes..................		14.700	0.425	1.911
		Lamp of 1st order, 23 burners, with 2 panes..................		17.000	0.435	1.953
		Lamp of 1st order, 23 burners, with 1 pane		21.000	0.445	2.026
5	Jan. 23, 1861, (during 9 hours.)	Lens of fixed light, 1st order.....		300.000	0.520	3.045
		Lens with electric light		2500.000	0.600	3.842
6	Jan. 29, 1861...	Small lamp......................		0.600	0.023	3.055
		Carcel lamp, unity..............		1.000	0.025	3.204
		Double-burner lamp.............		3.100	0.028	3.597
7	Feb. 4, 1861....	Robert lamp, with an elevation of flame of—	33mm	0.063	0.740	$\bar{1}.061$
			45mm	0.100	0.870	$\bar{1}.121$
			55mm	0.140	0.915	$\bar{1}.223$
			75mm	0.170	1.005	$\bar{1}.226$

A graphical construction has appeared to be the most convenient method for exhibiting a recapitulation of the facts stated, and leading to practical conclusions. From the relation

$$\frac{L a^x}{x^2} = \lambda$$

we deduce

$$\log \frac{L}{x^2} = x\,(-\log a) + \log \lambda,$$

and, if we represent each observation by a point having for abscissa the value found for x, and for ordinate that of $\log \frac{L}{x^2}$ which corresponds to it, all the points belonging to one and the same experiment, that is to say, the one state of atmosphere, ought to be situated upon a right line, of which the angle with the axis of x will have — log a for trigonometrical tangent, and the ordinate at the origin will be equal to log λ. That ordinate should be the same for all the right lines, if the observations were all made by persons endowed with the same acuteness of vision.

FIG. 1.

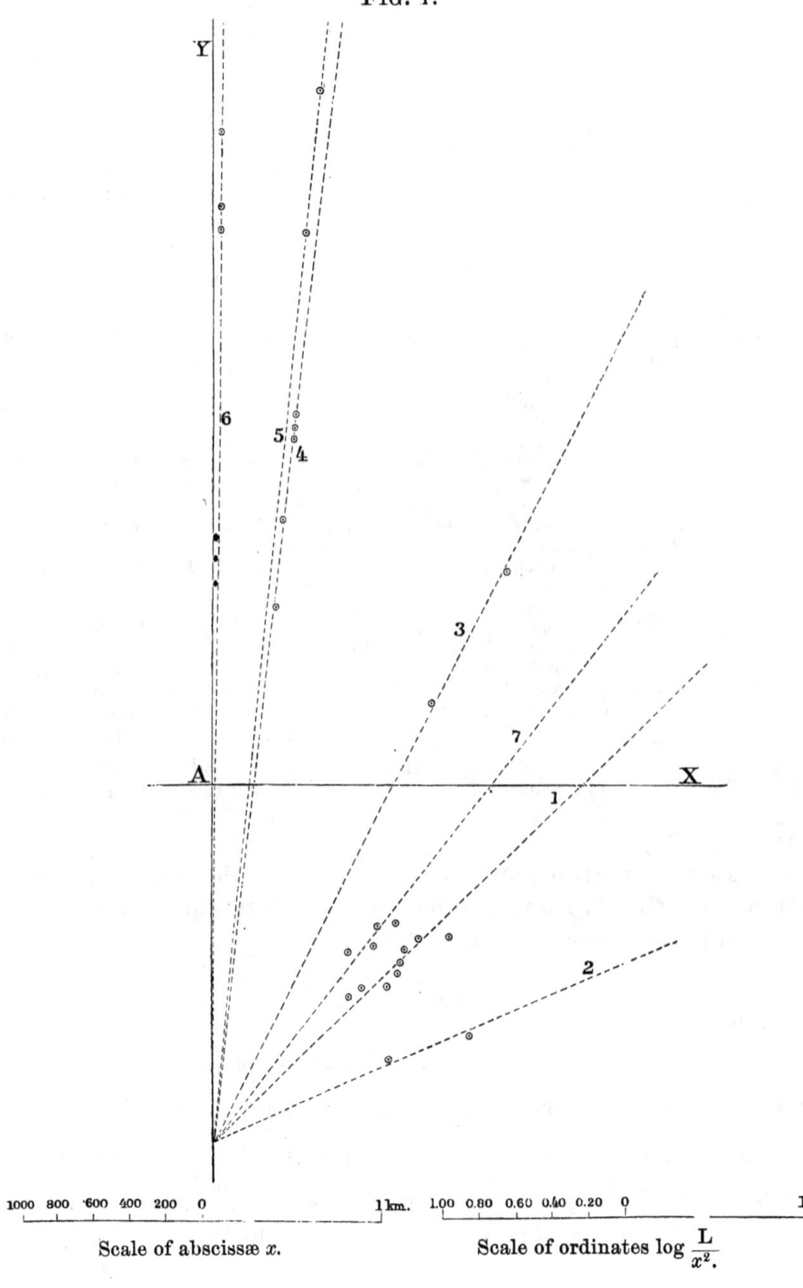

The figure preceding is the graphic representation referred to. It has been drawn on a scale of 0.025 of a meter to one. The points of construction are enclosed by small circles, and each of the lines carries the number assigned in the preceding table of the experiments, which express the conclusions.

There is, without doubt, something a little arbitrary in the tracing of these lines; there are some drawn in the direction which had been given to them. The observations lead rather beyond what the precise figures show, and that could hardly be otherwise, as well on account of the variations of the luminous intensity of the lights (foci) as in regard to the indecision which exists when it becomes necessary to fix a limit to the visibility. However, it is seen that the different lines deflect sufficiently little from the points where they should have been found in their course, if the experiments were made with rigorous exactness, and that they all unite in the same point of the axis of the ordinates. The height of this point of concurrence gives the value, log $\lambda = - 2.00$ from whence $\lambda = 0.010$.

The circumstances under which the observations were made would seem to establish the fact that this value of λ may be admitted in practice without the risk of errors. There were always three, and sometimes four, observers, and all wore spectacles but two. A mechanician employed in the operations, and possessing an excellent vision, continued constantly to observe the lights at the times when the observers were agreed that they had disappeared. Finally, some gas lamps were lighted upon the perimeter of the Champ de Mars, and even near the lights under observation, for experiment, and the contrast, as well as the fatigue of the eyes which observed without cessation the lights, more or less intense, must have injured the delicacy of their perception. The same persons could have seen the lights at a greater distance, and found consequently a smaller value for λ, if they had observed them in a space not illuminated by street lamps, or with visual organs in greater repose or less fatigued.

The preceding results have been verified by observations made at many of our light-houses. These observations certainly do not allow the assignment of a value to the coefficient under consideration, for the reason that the degree of transparency of the atmosphere at the moment when the proceeding takes place is ignored, but they suffice to establish the fact that the figures 0.010 may not be regarded as a minimum.

The following table is a recapitulation of some of them:

Place of observation.	Light-house observed.		Distance from place of observation.		Maximum value of λ, a being equal to—	
	Name.	Intensity by carcel burners.	Miles.	Kilometers.	0.973.	1.00.
Mont d'Agde	Cape Bearn......	600	50.00	92.60	0.005548	0.069972
Do.........	La Nouvelle	16	25.75	47.69	0.001907	0.007035
Cape Fréhel.....	Binic.............	16	20.50	37.97	0.003925	0.011098
Do.........	Ile Harbour	14	19.50	36.11	0.003996	0.010737
Do.........	Granville, (light-house.)	80	29.50	54.63	0.006009	0.026805
Baleines, (Ile de Ré.)	Sables-d'Olonn (harbor light.)	16	17.50	32.41	0.006273	0.015232
Bréhat, (Pointe du Paon.)	Ile Harbour	14	13.83	25.61	0.010589	0.021345

The first column shows the place of observation; the second, the name of the light; the third, the intensity of the light; the fourth, the distance at which it is sometimes seen; the fifth, assigns a high limit to the value of λ, in the double hypothesis that the coefficient of transparency of atmosphere had, at the moment of the observations, the value of 0.973 which Bouguer assigned to it, and that it was equal to unity; that is to say, that a complete transparency of atmosphere existed at the time the observations were made. It has been calculated from the formula given above—

$$\lambda = L \frac{a^x}{x^2}.$$

It is seen that, if the coefficient of Bouguer be adopted, all these observations, except the last, give the figures notably lower than 0.010, and that one of them brings λ below 0.007, when it was at the same time admitted that the atmosphere was perfectly transparent. It is also to be observed, that these figures are the *maxima*, as the lights were in sight, and some of them reported as very brilliant at the moment the observations were recorded. The observations made upon the light of the Isle Harbour took place during the months of December, 1860, and January and February, 1861, establishing the fact that the light was seen during forty-five nights, and that it was found very brilliant twenty-one times. The light of Nouvelle, which gives the lowest figure, has not been seen, on the other hand, but fourteen times in nine years, but it is but just to add that the keepers of the light of Agde never observed it but from the interior of their lantern, and did not attach any great importance to having discovered it. Besides, this figure is, under every hypothesis, below that which we have admitted.

This being stated, let us return to the study of the result of the experiments made in the Champ de Mars. The value of λ being considered as determined with a sufficient rigor in regard to the delicateness of the visual organs of the observers, we may deduce from the formula by the method of least squares, or, more simply, by measures taken from the figure, the approximate values of a, which correspond to the different series of observations.

But some of these expressions of a show, that if the means adopted to define the degree of transparency of the atmosphere is irreproachable, in a purely scientific point of view, it leaves much to be desired in practice, on account of the number of figures or of the form which it exacts during the prevalence of dense fogs. Thus, log a has 9 for its characteristic on the 23d of January, and more than 200 on the 29th of the same month. And, on the other hand, it should not be forgotten, that the coefficient a does not represent sufficiently to the mind the atmospheric circumstances of which it gives a rigorous definition.

But all these inconveniences will disappear, if the degree of transparency of the atmosphere is expressed by the range of the unity of light to the unity of distance, for an observer of ordinary vision, which is represented by the $\lambda = 0.010$ with the kilometer for unity. The value of this new coefficient will be deduced from the formula—

$$a^{p} = 0.010\, p^{2},$$

which gives $p = 10.00$ for $a = 1$, that is to say, in the case of a completely transparent atmosphere, and $p = 8.859$ for $a = 0.973$, the coefficient assigned by Bouguer. From the experiment made on the 29th January it may be concluded that $p = 0.025$, the 23d of the same month the mean value of p has passed from 0.329 to 0.309.

The relation $L \frac{a^{x}}{x^{2}} = \lambda$ shows how the ranges vary with the luminous intensities of the focus and the degree of transparency of the atmosphere, and it becomes very expressive in a graphic interpretation. The curves of Plate 2 correspond each to a determined value of a and of p. Those of Figure 1 have been traced in carrying the luminous intensities upon the axis of the abscissæ to the scale of 0.005*m.* for 1,000 burners, and the ranges upon the axis of the ordinates to the scale of 0.02 *m.* for 100 kilometers. The Figure 2 is executed upon a larger scale, to the tenthfold; it is only an amplification of the square comprised between the dotted lines upon the Figure 1, but it gives a larger number of curves.

The upper curve in each figure belongs to $a = 1$; it is a parabola. The last curve of Figure 2 belongs to an atmosphere the coefficient of whose transparency will be equal to 0.00000625, that is to say, in which the light of unity will not reach farther than 500 meters.

It will be seen immediately, by an inspection of the figures, and especially of the first, in what very great proportion the luminous ranges are reduced by the defect of atmospheric transparency, however little marked it may be. When there is sufficient fog to prevent a carcel lamp from being seen at a greater distance than 1,000 meters, there is not a sensible difference in the graphic expression between the range of a light equivalent to 4,000 burners and that of a light five times more intense. The calculation gives 2.42*km.* in the first case, and 2.72*km.* in the second.

The range of a light of 4,000 burners, which will be 632 kilometers in a vacuum, becomes reduced to 98 in an atmosphere of 0.962, and falls to 16 when this coefficient descends to 0.632, which is not rare, inasmuch as the unity light is seen then at 4,000 meters distance. It is not more than 1.07*km.*, when that last distance is reduced to 500 meters. It is seen, also, that the curves approach each other much more rapidly from a parallel to the axis of the abscissæ, as the value of a is smaller, and it may be concluded from that, that within a certain limit, there is no very great necessity for increasing the intensity of the focus.

This last order of considerations is very important, and it may be remarked in regard to it that it is outside of all hypothesis. An altogether different value for λ might be adopted, as the conclusion will be the same.

The equation of the ranges is not one of easy application, in that it requires long calculations for determining x, which is the value which it is usually proposed to obtain; but it may be replaced by the graphic constructions, from which will be immediately obtained the solutions sought, with all the rigorous correctness which is practically required; and even the curves which the reader has before his eyes give indications which will appear to be sufficient in the greater number of circumstances and cases.

It is doubtless unnecessary to insist further upon this subject, and we will proceed to examine now how the points which have just been established allow the fixing of the luminous ranges to be assigned to the apparatus of the different orders.

They cannot be determined in an absolute manner; they are necessarily the function of a certain state of the atmosphere. To take the coefficient 0.973 of Bouguer, would not do for habitual circumstances; to descend to a very low figure would be to remove it outside of the limits which actually exist, and would give a false idea of the power of our maritime illumination. There would be no advantage in taking this last position, for navigators know full well that they cannot count upon the admitted ranges when the atmosphere is foggy. We have stopped at the figure 0.903, which corresponds to the range of 7 kilometers of the light of unity, and which appears to represent a mean state of the atmosphere in our climates.

INTENSITIES AND LUMINOUS RANGES.

The table which follows shows the luminous intensities upon which it is allowed to count in practice, and the corresponding ranges in three states of the atmosphere, which are defined by the expressions $a = 0.966$, $a = 0.903$, and $a = 747$. From the observations made at our lights, it seems to be established, that along the whole of our seacoast the mean transparency of the atmosphere is greater during one month than is indicated by the first of these figures, during six months than is indicated by the second, and during eleven months than is indicated by the last. In the last column of the table are inserted the amplitudes, at the moment of emerging from the apparatus, of the flashes of the eclipse lights, and of those which illuminate only a part of the horizon. Only white lights are considered, and it will be found further on in what proportion it will be proper to reduce the figures of the intensities to apply them to colored lights.

TABLE OF INTENSITIES AND LUMINOUS RANGES.

Designation of the Illuminating Apparatus.	Intensity in carcel burners.		Range in nautical miles, in an atmosphere represented by—						Amplitude of the flash in degrees and tenths of degrees.
			$a=0.966$ $p=8630\,m.$		$a=0.903$ $p=7000\,m.$		$a=0.747$ $p=4900\,m.$		
	Of fixed light.	Of the flash.	Fixed light.	Flash.	Fixed light.	Flash.	Fixed light.	Flash.	
APPARATUS OF THE 1ST ORDER, *With lamp consumtng 760 gr. colza oil per hour, and supplying 23 burners.*									
Fixed light	630	......	39.3	......	20.2	......	9.8	......	......
Light with eclipses from minute to minute (Lenses $\frac{1}{8}$; prolonged flashes.)	60	5075	21.3	59.3	12.7	27.9	6.8	12.7	9.4
Light with eclipses from 30″ to 30″ (Lenses $\frac{1}{16}$; prolonged flashes.)	60	2525	21.3	52.2	12.7	25.2	6.8	11.7	9.4
Light with eclipses from 30″ to 30″ (Lenses $\frac{1}{16}$; short flashes.)	60	3475	21.3	55.4	12.7	26.4	6.8	12.1	6.0
Light with eclipses from 20″ to 20″ and less (Lenses $\frac{1}{24}$; short flashes.)	......	2450	......	51.9	......	25.1	......	11.6	6.0
Fixed light varied by flashes, (movable lenses of 35° 12′)	630 190	4000	39.3 29.4	56.8	20.2 16.2	27.0	9.8 8.2	12.3	5.6
APPARATUS OF THE 2D ORDER, *With lamp consuming 500 gr. colza oil per hour, and supplying 15 burners.*									
Fixed light	335	......	33.9	......	18.0	......	8.9	......	......
Light with eclipses from minute to minute (Lenses $\frac{1}{8}$; prolonged flashes.)	25	2550	16.2	52.3	10.3	25.3	5.8	11.7	9.4
Light with eclipses from 30″ to 30″ (Lenses $\frac{1}{12}$; prolonged flashes.)	25	1675	16.2	48.2	10.3	23.7	5.8	11.1	9.4

Light with eclipes from 30″ to 30″ (Lenses $\frac{1}{12}$; short flashes.)	25	2275	16.2	51.2	10.3	24.8	5.8	11.5	6.0
Light with eclipses from 20″ to 20″ and less (Lenses $\frac{1}{20}$; short flashes.)		1450		46.9		23.2		10.9	6.0
Fixed light varied by flashes, (movable lenses of 43° 40′)	335 95	2700	33.9 24.4	52.9	18.0 14.0	25.5	8.9 7.3	11.8	5.3
Apparatus of the 3d order, *With lamp consuming* 175 *gr. colza oil per hour, and supplying* 5 *burners.*									
Fixed light	90		24.0		13.9		7.3		
Light with eclipses from minute to minute (Lenses $\frac{1}{8}$; prolonged flashes.)	7	845	10.3	41.9	7.2	21.2	4.4	10.2	8.5
Light with eclipses from 30″ to 30″ (Lenses $\frac{1}{12}$; prolonged flashes.)	7	550	10.3	38.1	7.2	19.7	4.4	9.6	8.5
Light with eclipses from 30″ to 30″ (Lenses $\frac{1}{12}$; short flashes.)	7	750	10.3	40.8	7.2	20.8	4.4	10.0	5.5
Light with eclipses from 20″ to 20″ and less (Lenses $\frac{1}{16}$; short flashes.		590		38.7		20.0		9.7	5.5
Light with flashes from 20″ to 20″, without eclipses (Lenses $\frac{1}{10}$.)	50	470	20.2	36.7	12.2	19.2	6.6	9.4	5.2
Fixed light varied by flashes, (movable lenses of 44° 32′)	90 25	950	24.0 16.2	42.9	13.9 10.3	21.6	7.3 5.8	10.3	4.7
Apparatus of the 3d order, (small pattern,) *With lamp consuming* 110 *gr. colza oil per hour, and supplying* 3 *burners.*									
Fixed light	30		17.2		10.8		6.0		
Light with eclipses from minute to minute (Lenses $\frac{1}{6}$.)	6	275	9.7	32.4	6.9	17.4	4.2	8.7	9.0
Light with eclipses from 30″ to 30″ and less (Lenses $\frac{1}{10}$.)	6	165	9.7	28.3	6.9	15.7	4.2	8.0	9.0
Fixed light varied by flashes, (movable lenses of 50°)	30 8.5	238	17.2 11.1	31.2	10.8 7.7	16.9	6.0 4.6	8.5	7.0

TABLE OF INTENSITIES AND LUMINOUS RANGES—CONTINUED.

Designation of the Illuminating Apparatus.	Intensity in carcel burners.		Range in nautical miles, in an atmosphere represented by—						Amplitude of the flash in degrees and tenths of degrees.
	Of fixed light.	Of the flash.	$a=0.966$ $p=8630m.$		$a=0.903$ $p=7000m.$		$a=0.747$ $p=4900m.$		
			Fixed light.	Flash.	Fixed light.	Flash.	Fixed light.	Flash.	
APPARATUS OF THE 4TH ORDER, *Of* 0.375*m. in diameter.*									
Fixed light, with lamp for colza oil, consuming 60 gr. per hour, and supplying 1*b*. 6	13	....	12.9	....	8.6	....	5.0	....	......
Fixed light, with lamp for schist oil, consuming 65 gr. per hour, and supplying 2*b*. 2	24	....	16.0	....	10.2	....	5.7	....	......
Light varied by flashes, with lamp for colza oil of 1*b*. 6, (movable lenses of 61° 34′)	13 3.7	118	12.9 8.1	25.9	8.6 5.9	14.7	5.0 3.8	7.6	7.0
Light varied by flashes, with lamp for schist oil of 2*b*. 2, (movable lenses of 61° 34′)	24 6.5	221	16.0 10.0	30.6	10.2 7.1	16.7	5.7 4.3	8.4	7.0
APPARATUS OF THE 4TH ORDER, *Of* 0.30*m. in diameter.*									
Fixed light, with lamp for colza oil, consuming 50 gr. per hour, and supplying 1*b*. 3	9	....	11.3	....	7.8	....	4.6	....	......
Fixed light, with lamp for schist oil, consuming 65 gr. per hour, and supplying 2*b*. 2	18	....	14.5	....	9.4	....	5.4	....	......
Fixed light, in cut glass or in cast class for hanging lanterns, with lamp of 1*b*. 3	6	....	9.7	....	6.9	....	4.2	....	......
APPARATUS FOR RANGE LIGHTS.									
Lens in cast glass, of 1 meter in diameter, with lamp of 1*b*. 6	200	....	29.8	....	16.4	....	8.3	....	12.0
Lens in cut glass, of 0.50*m*. in diameter, with lamp of 1*b*. 6	300	....	33.0	....	17.7	....	8.8	....	9.0

Reflector, aperture of 0. 85*m*., with lamp consuming 175 gr. per hour, and supplying 5 burners	760	....	40. 9	....	20. 8	....	10. 0	....	18. 0
Reflector, aperture of 0. 85*m*., with lamp consuming 60 gr. per hour, and suppiying 1*b*. 6	550	....	38. 1	....	19. 7	....	9. 6	....	12. 0
Reflector, aperture of 0. 50*m*., with lamp consuming 60 gr. per hour, and supplying 1*b*. 6	200	....	29. 8	....	16. 4	....	8. 3	....	20. 0
Photophore, aperture of 0. 29*m*., with lamp consuming 50 gr. per hour, and supplying 1*b*. 3	60	....	21. 3	....	12. 7	....	6. 8	....	36. 0
SIDEREAL APPARATUS.									
Sidereal large burner, with lamp consuming 45 gr. per hour, and supplying 1*b*. 15	3. 5	....	7. 9	....	5. 8	....	3. 7	....	....

REMARKS.—Photometric measurements give much greater intensities than those in the table. Account has been taken of the practical imperfections and of the absorption of the luminous rays by the plate glass of the lantern. Account has also been taken of the increased intensity which is obtained in collecting, by means of spherical reflectors, the luminous rays which diverge uselessly to the earth. The lights varied by flashes present two lights fixed. The one the most intense is seen during the major part of the time; the other is seen during the eclipses. The ranges assigned to these lights are those of the principal fixed light.

Plate 1 represents in a very striking manner the luminous intensities of our principal illuminating apparatus, and the corresponding ranges, in an atmosphere in a mean state, that which gives to the light of unity a range of 7 kilometers. The drawings which form the lower series of figures show the general dispositions of the apparatus and the directions they give to the luminous rays. The curves of the upper series represent the intensities; they have the durations of the luminous appearances for abscissæ to the scale of 0.03*m.* per minute, and the intensities for ordinates to the scale of 0.004*m.* per one hundred burners. The figures relating to the ranges occupy the intermediate spaces; they are drawn to the scale of 0.001 per nautical mile, or of 0.00054*m.* per kilometer. It has been sought to render an account, in these last figures, of the variation of the luminous intensity, which is not the same in the whole illuminated zone.*

On the inspection of that figure, the reader will doubtless be much more impressed than he has been by the preceding calculations, or even by the curves of Plate 2, with the small augmentation of range which corresponds to a marked increase of intensity after it reaches a certain limit.

GEOGRAPHICAL RANGES.

The distance at which a light-house may be seen is limited more precisely by the spheroidal form of the earth than by the intensity of the light at the burner or focus. The geographical range depends upon the height of the light above the level of the sea, upon the radius of

FIG. 2.

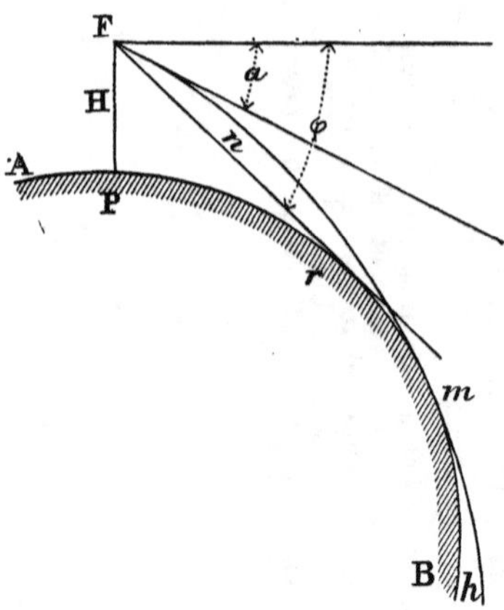

* The conception of this last mode of representation belongs to Mr. Allard, the Engineer-in-chief, and they have been executed under his direction.

curvature of that part of the earth's surface at which it is placed, and upon the value of the atmospheric refraction.

The luminous rays which traverse the atmosphere come in contact with strata of air whose density diminishes in proportion to their elevation; they meet successive refractions, and describe, consequently, curves, when they are not directed normally to the surface of the earth. These curves are concave below, and the refraction has the effect of increasing the ranges, as is shown by Figure 2.

Let A B be the surface of the sea, F the focal point, P F its height, F *n m* the curve, which is tangent to the surface of the sea at *m*, F *r* the tangent from the point F. The geographical range will be equal to P *m*, whilst it would have only P *r* for its value, if there had been no refraction. The luminous ray, which, departing from the point F, directed tangentially to the surface, makes, with the horizontal line traced in the same plane, an angle a, which is less than the angle φ of the tangent F *r* with the same line.

The atmospheric refraction is not constant, but in questions of that kind a mean value may be readily admitted, and deduce the ranges from the formula

$$D = \sqrt{\frac{R\,H}{0.42}}$$

in which H is the height above the level of the high water, and R the radius of curvature of the surface. For this last coefficient the value $R = 6366953m.$ has been adopted. This represents the radius of curvature of the meridian at the latitude of 45° 44′, which may be considered as the mean for the lights on our seacoasts.

The results deduced from that formula give the geographical ranges, in supposing that the eye of the observer is placed at the level of the sea. If it were elevated to a height h above that surface, it would extend the tangent point, without losing sight of the light, until at a distance equal to $\sqrt{\frac{R\,h}{0.42}}$. The general formula for ranges is, then,

$$P = \sqrt{\frac{R\,H}{0.42}} + \sqrt{\frac{R\,h}{0.42}}.$$

There is another element which belongs to the same question, and which is very necessary to be taken into consideration in establishing illuminating apparatus; it is the angle, a, which the tangent to the curve at the point, F, forms with the horizon, since that is the direction in which the most intense luminous beam should be directed. This subject will be returned to when the question of the disposition of the apparatus comes up.

The following table shows, in kilometers and nautical miles, the geographical ranges corresponding to different heights above the level of the sea, both for the focal point and the eye of the observer.

TABLE OF GEOGRAPHICAL RANGES.

Height of centre of the flame above the level of the sea.	Distance of the point of contact of the luminous ray tangent to the surface of the sea, $D = \sqrt{\frac{R. H.}{0.42.}}$ R = 6,366,953.		GEOGRAPHICAL RANGES For an observer of whose height *h*, above the level of the sea, is equal to—											
			3*m*.		6*m*.		9*m*.		12*m*.		15*m*.		20*m*.	
	In meters.	In miles.	In meters.	In miles.	In meters.	In miles.	In meters.	In miles.	In meters.	In miles.	In meters.	In miles.	In meters.	In miles.
1	3,894	2.10	10,638	5.74	13,431	7.25	15,575	8.41	17,382	9.39	18,973	10.25	21,306	11.51
2	5,506	2.97	12,250	6.62	15,043	8.12	17,187	9.28	18,994	10.26	20,585	11.12	22,918	12.38
3	6,744	3.64	13,488	7.28	16,281	8.79	18,425	9.95	20,232	10.93	21,823	11.78	24,156	13.04
4	7,787	4.20	14,531	7.85	17,324	9.35	19,468	10.51	21,275	11.49	22,866	12.35	25,199	13.61
5	8,706	4.70	15,450	8.34	18,243	9.85	20,387	11.01	22,194	11.98	23,785	12.84	26,118	14.10
6	9,537	5.15	16,281	8.79	19,074	10.30	21,218	11.46	23,025	12.43	24,616	13.29	26,949	14.55
7	10,301	5.56	17,045	9.20	19,838	10.71	21,982	11,87	23,789	12.85	25,380	13.71	27,713	14.97
8	11,013	5.95	17,757	9.59	20,550	11.10	22,694	12.25	24,501	13.23	26,092	14.09	28,425	15.35
9	11,681	6.31	18,425	9.95	21,218	11.46	23,362	12.62	25,169	13.59	26,760	14.45	29,093	15.71
10	12,312	6.65	19,056	10.29	21,849	11.80	23,993	12.96	25,800	13.93	27,391	14.79	29,724	16.05
11	12,913	6.97	19,657	10.61	22,450	12.12	24,594	13.28	26,401	14.26	27,992	15.12	30,325	16.38
12	13,488	7.28	20,232	10.93	23,025	12.43	25,169	13.59	26,976	14.57	28,567	15.43	30,900	16.69
13	14,038	7.58	20,782	11.22	23,575	12.73	25,719	13.89	27,526	14.86	29,117	15.72	31,450	16.98
14	14,568	7.87	21,312	11.51	24,105	13.02	26,249	14.17	28,056	15.15	29,647	16.01	31,980	17.27
15	15,079	8.14	21,823	11.78	24,616	13.29	26,760	14.45	28,567	15.43	30,158	16.29	32,491	17.55
20	17,412	9.40	24,156	13.04	26,949	14.55	29,093	15.71	30,900	16.69	32,491	17.55	34,824	18.80
25	19,468	10.51	26,212	14.15	29,005	15.66	31,149	16.82	32,956	17.80	34,547	18.65	36,880	19.92
30	21,326	11.52	28,070	15.16	30,863	16.67	33,007	17.82	34,814	18.80	36,405	19.66	38,738	20.92
35	23,034	12.44	29,778	16.08	32,571	17.59	34,715	18.75	36,522	19.72	38,113	20.58	40,446	21.84
40	24,625	13.30	31,369	16.94	34,162	18.45	36,306	19.61	38,113	20.58	39,704	21.44	42,037	22.70
45	26,118	14.10	32,862	17.75	35,655	19.25	37,799	20.41	39,606	21.39	41,197	22.25	43,530	23.51
50	27,531	14.87	34,275	18.51	37,068	20.02	39,212	21.17	41,019	22.15	42,610	23.01	44,943	24.27
55	28,875	15.59	35,619	19.23	38,412	20.74	40,556	21.90	42,363	22.88	43,954	23.74	46,287	24.99
60	30,159	16.29	36,903	19.93	39,696	21.44	41,840	22.59	43,647	23.59	45,238	24.43	47,571	25.69

65	31,390	16.95	38,134	20.59	40,927	22.10	43,071	23.26	44,878	24.23	46,469	25,09	48,802	26.35
70	32,575	17.59	39,319	21.23	42,112	22.74	44,256	23.90	46,063	24.87	47,654	25.73	49,987	26.99
75	33,719	18.21	40,463	21.85	43,256	23.36	45,400	24.52	47,207	25.49	48,798	26.35	51,131	27.61
80	34,825	18.81	41,579	22.45	44,362	23.96	46,506	25.11	48,313	26.09	49,904	26.95	52,237	28.21
85	35,896	19.38	42,640	23.03	45,433	24.53	47,577	25.69	49,384	26.67	50,975	27.53	53,308	28.79
90	36,937	19.95	43,681	23.59	46,474	25.10	48,618	26.25	50,425	27.23	52,016	28.09	54,349	29.35
95	37,949	20.49	44,693	24.13	47,486	25.64	49,630	26.80	51,437	27.78	53,028	28.64	55,361	29.89
100	38,935	21.02	45,679	24.67	48,472	26.17	50,616	27.33	52,423	28.31	54,014	29.17	56,347	30.43
110	40,835	22.05	47,579	25.69	50,372	27.20	52,516	28.36	54,323	29.33	55,914	30.19	58,247	31.45
120	42,651	23.03	49,395	26.67	52,188	28.18	54,332	29.34	56,139	30.32	57,730	31.17	60,063	32.43
130	44,393	23.97	51,137	27.61	53,930	29.12	56,074	30.28	57,881	31.26	59,472	32.11	61,805	33.37
140	46,069	24.88	52,813	28.52	55,606	30.03	57,750	31.19	59,557	32.16	61,148	33.02	63,481	34.28
150	47,686	25.75	54,430	29.39	57,223	30.90	59,367	32.06	61,174	33.03	62.765	33.89	65,098	35.15
160	49,249	26.59	55,993	30.24	58,786	31.74	69,930	32.90	62,737	33.88	64,328	34.74	66,661	36.00
170	50,765	27.41	57,509	31.05	60,302	32.56	62,446	33.72	64,253	34.70	65,844	35.56	68,177	36.82
180	52,237	28.21	58,981	31.85	61,774	33.36	63.918	34.52	65,725	35.49	67,316	36.35	69,649	37.61
190	53,668	28.98	60,412	32.62	63,205	34.13	65,349	35.29	67,156	36.26	68,747	37.12	71,080	38.38
200	55,063	29.73	61,807	33.38	64,600	34.88	66,744	36,04	68,551	37.02	70,142	37.88	72,475	39.14
220	57.750	31.19	64,494	34.83	67,287	36.33	69,431	37.49	71,238	38.47	72,829	39.33	75,162	40.59
240	60,318	32.57	67,062	36.21	69,855	37.72	71,999	38.88	73,806	39.86	75,397	40.71	77,730	41.97
260	62,781	33.90	69,525	37.54	72,318	39.05	74,462	40.21	76,269	41.19	77,860	42.04	80,193	43.30
280	65,151	35.18	71,895	38.82	74,688	40.33	76,832	41.49	78,639	42.47	80,230	43.32	82,563	44.58
300	67,438	36.42	74,182	40.06	76,975	41.57	79,119	42.72	80,926	43.70	82,517	44.56	84,850	45.82

All of our lights are not placed on a sufficiently great elevation to be seen as far as the limit of the ranges assigned to them by an observer from the deck of a vessel, and the numbers of this table, or, in their default, the formula from which they have been derived, allows the recognition of the point at which it is necessary to be elevated above the level of the sea to observe at the horizon a light whose position is known with reference to the same plane. Navigators may thus judge approximately at what distance they are from a light at the moment it appears to come up out of the sea. The heights of the light-houses being given in the lists and nautical books, with reference to the level of the highest water,* it will become necessary, in order to proceed with exactness, to add to the height of the light-house seen the difference between that level and that of the sea at the moment the observation is made.

Thus, let us suppose it should be necessary to have an elevation of 12 meters above the level of the sea to see a light whose height is 42 meters emerge, and that, at the moment of observation, the level of the water is 3 meters below that of the highest tides, it will be found from the table that the distance is 21.39 miles from the foot of the tower. This is certainly not a method of rigorous exactitude, but it will be readily seen that approximate results are quite admissible in such a matter.

IV.—RELATIVE POSITIONS OF MULTIPLE LIGHTS.

The association of lights together at any one station has two distinct objects—either to produce a very marked characteristic distinction, or to serve as a range line to avoid dangers. In the first case, the distance between the lights to be observed from a distance should be such as to prevent their being blended into or supposed to be one light at any distance within the limits of their range; in the second, they must be so arranged that the navigator will always see them separated, and perceive the moment he departs from the straight range line they are placed to mark; that is to say, to enable him to discover any departure from that line before he runs into those dangers which these lights are placed to guide clear of.

The elements of the question are limited to the phenomena of the irradiation, when it is simply proposed to obtain a distinctive character; but when it becomes a question of range lights, it will be necessary, besides, to make the range line so direct that it may be caught by a glance of the observer, or, in other words, the value of the angle which ought to make in horizontal projection two luminous points situated at different heights, so that men who are little accustomed to forming estimates of the kind may see at once that these luminous points are

* The light-house list of the United States gives the heights to mean low tide.—T. A. J.

not placed upon one and the same elevation. The two problems ought, then, to be considered separately.

IRRADIATION.

It is known that the amplitude of the irradiation depends upon three things—the luminous intensity of the object, the darkness of the back ground upon which it is projected, and the degree of shortsightedness of the observer. It increases with each of them.

EFFECTS OF SHORTSIGHTEDNESS.

In order to illustrate this last point more definitely, we will cite the following experiments made upon the gas lamps of the city of Paris, by four persons of different powers of vision. These lights, placed on two sides of a bridge, were observed from one of the adjacent quays, which extended in a right line. The observers withdrew from the bridge and marked the points where the luminous halos, which to their eyes encircled two lamps opposite to each other, appeared to them tangent, yet leaving the lights perfectly distinct to their vision.

Three of these observers were shortsighted, and the numbers of the glasses required by them were No. 8 for the first, No. 11 for the second, and No. 16 for the third. They did not on this occasion use glasses. The fourth had excellent sight. The distances at which the lights were observed varied from 95 to 626 meters; the night was dark, the atmos phere very clear, and distance does not seem (between these limits) to have had any appreciable influence upon the phenomenon. Each person made several observations, agreeing within a few minutes. The mean results of the observations gave the following for the size of the apparent irradiations:

1st observer	1°	12′	15″
2d observer	1	7	22
3d observer		57	7
4th observer		12	0

It is thus seen how important it is that near-sighted persons should not be employed as pilots.*

The more important experiments which follow were made by persons who had good sight, or wore spectacles to assure it. Two men who possessed remarkably acute sight took part in the work, but did not think proper to submit their observations, because they were considered as belonging to exceptional organizations. They only served to establish the fact that the other observers were within the ordinary conditions found in practice.

* It is to be remarked that spectacles, which so well assist that infirmity under ordinary circumstances, are but an insufficient palliative at sea, where the glasses soon become covered with moisture, or with crystals of salt, and thus lose their clearness.

ANGLES OF BLENDING OF THE LIGHTS.

The first trial was to determine the smallest angle under which two lights ought to be seen to appear markedly distinct.

Trial was made in succession with carcel lamps, apparatus of 0.30*m*. diameter, parabolic reflectors of 0.29*m*. of opening, lenses of fixed-light apparatus of the first order, and with large annular lenses of the same class. The observers, to the number of three, placed themselves at different distances from the lights, and indicated, by means of signals previously agreed upon, the direction in which the illuminating apparatus placed upon a horizontal track should be moved. They always agreed in their estimations. The night was dark, and the atmosphere clear. The following table will show the results obtained:

Apparatus.	Luminous intensity. Total.	Luminous intensity. Per square centimeter.	Separation of the lights.	Distance of observers.	Visual angle.	Appearance of the lights.
			m.	*m.*	′ ″	
Carcel lamps	1*b*.	0*b*.11	0.90	965	3.12	Almost blended.
			0.90	1004	3.5	Blended.
			0.90	500	6.11	Sufficiently distinct.
			1.00	1004	3 25	Almost blended.
			1.00	1300	2.39	Blended.
			1.00	610	5.38	Sufficiently distinct.
			1.10	725	5.13	The same.
			1.20	810	5.6	The same.
			1 30	850	5.15	The same.
			1.40	965	4.59	The same.
Catadioptric apparatus of 0.30*m*	10	0 125	1.00	772	4.27	Almost blended.
			1.00	600	5.44	Not sufficiently distinct.
			1.20	1407	2.56	Blended.
			1.20	600	6.52	Sufficiently distinct.
			1.50	772	6.41	The same.
White parabolic reflectors	80	0.13	1.00	1030	3.20	Blended.
			1.40	675	7.8	Not sufficiently distinct.
			1.50	675	7.38	Sufficiently distinct.
Parabolic reflectors, with lights colored red by means of a sheet of glass	....	....	1.50	850	6.4	The same.
A parabolic reflector white, and a red one	....	....	1.40	772	6.14	The same.
			1.30	772	5.47	Not sufficiently distinct.
			1.10	590	6.25	Sufficiently distinct.
			1.00	500	6.52	The same.
			0.90	500	6.11	Not sufficiently distinct.
Lamps of 1st order, with dioptric lenses to fixed light of one meter in height	400	0.44	2.90	673	14.49	Sufficiently distinct.
			4.40	1154	13.6	Not quite distinct enough.
			3.70	1154	11.1	Not sufficiently distinct.
Lamps of 1st order, with annular lenses of one meter in height, embracing the 8th of the circumference	3000	0.43	2.00	800	8.36	Almost blended.
			3.00	800	12.53	Not quite distinct enough.
			3.00	700	14.44	Very distinct.
			3.24	772	14.26	Sufficiently distinct.
			3.74	890	14.27	The same.
			4.14	1004	14.11	The same.
			4.50	1100	14.4	The same.
			3.00	1407	7.20	Complete confusion.
			5.00	1407	12 13	Not sufficiently distinct.
			6.00	1407	14.40	Sufficiently distinct.
			6.00	2750	7.30	Complete confusion.
			9.00	2750	11.15	Not sufficiently distinct.
			11.00	2750	13.45	Almost sufficiently distinct.
Lamps of 1st order, with annular lenses of one meter in height, embracing the 16th of the circumference	1500	0.43	2.00	1100	6.15	Complete confusion.
			4.50	1100	14.4	Sufficiently distinct.

It is seen that, excepting some slight anomalies, inherent in experiments of this sort, the irradiation augments, not with the power of the focus, but with the luminous intensity, by unity of surface of the illuminating body.

If the luminous intensities decreased in proportion to the square of the distance, the amplitude of the irradiation would be the same whatever might be the distance of the observer. But it is not so. The decrease is more rapid, and the irradiation diminishes with the distance in a proportion just so much greater as the atmosphere diminishes in clearness, except, however, during rain and thick fog, as has been established by observations, of which we will hereafter speak. It follows that the figures deduced from experiments which have not gone beyond 2,750 meters may be considered as *maxima*, with the benefit of that reservation, and to be regulated by them, would be making a quite prudent allowance. Nevertheless, the Lighting Service judged that it would be well to go further, and not wishing to enter into details which could not be easily reconciled with the exigencies of practice, and which would be of too absolute a character, it has fixed the following as the least angle which two lights ought to make in order to appear sufficiently distinct:

For beacons.......................................8′
For lights of the three largest orders....................15′

INFLUENCE OF THE STATE OF THE ATMOSPHERE.

Observations made from the sea upon multiple lights, and in different circumstances, established the fact that there need be no fear of mistake in relying upon these figures. They have shown, besides, that fog and rain exert upon the phenomena under discussion an influence which may be easily conceived, but which had not been well established. Although the lights lose part of their brilliancy in these states of the atmosphere, yet their irradiation appears to augment in a certain proportion. This may be attributed to the fact that those drops of rain or vecicles of fog nearest to the light are illuminated with sufficient vividness to send luminous rays to the observer, and increase in that way the dimensions of the illuminating body. Still, that irradiation does not exceed the limits which have just been stated.

Thus, the two tide-lights of the port of Boulogne, which are elevated three meters one above the other, have been distinguished at a distance of two miles in clear weather, and were blended at less than one and a half mile during a fog. They were seen, in the first case, under an angle of 2′ 47″, and in the second under an angle of 3′ 43″. These observations were made by a pilot who had good sight, as is proved by the small value of the angles under which the vision was distinct.

Thus, again, the two fixed lights of the first order, at the mouth of the Canche, are seen from the light at Alpreck, under an angle of 4′ 10″, at a distance of eleven and a half miles, and they appear distinct or blended according to the state of the atmosphere.

In 1,029 observations made during a course of one year, the lights were visible 206 times during fog, but they appeared distinct only 94 times, being 46 per cent; during rain they were seen 63 times, but appeared distinct but 14 times, being 22 per cent; during clear or clouded sky, without rain or apparent fog, they were seen 533 times, and remained distinct 409 times, being 77 per cent.

MULTIPLE LIGHTS.

These figures of 8′ for beacon-lights, and of 15′ for light-houses, being admitted, the solution of the problem of the establishment of multiple lights, with the view to constitute a distinctive characteristic, is very simple, especially when the simplifications which practice permits are introduced in the data.

Let M N (Fig. 3) be the portion of the shore line which it is designed to light, O the centre of the line which will join the two lights, the arc of the circle X Y Z the limit of the range of these lights, (arc described from the point O, and which may be substituted without sensible error for the near identical arcs drawn from each light as centres,) V O W the angle embracing all the directions in which a navigator has interest to recognize the character of the illumination of the point O, that is to say, where he may find himself in the presence of these lights before having seen any other. The line joining the lights ought to be perpendicular to the line bisecting the angle V O W, and, if we call x the distance A B of the two lights, p the line O V or the range, a the angle $VOY = \frac{VOW}{2}$, we will be able to lay down

$$x = 2p \frac{\sin 4'}{\cos a},$$

if it relates to simple beacon-lights, and

$$x = 2p \frac{\sin 7' 30''}{\cos a},$$

if more powerful lights constitute the illumination.

FIG. 3.

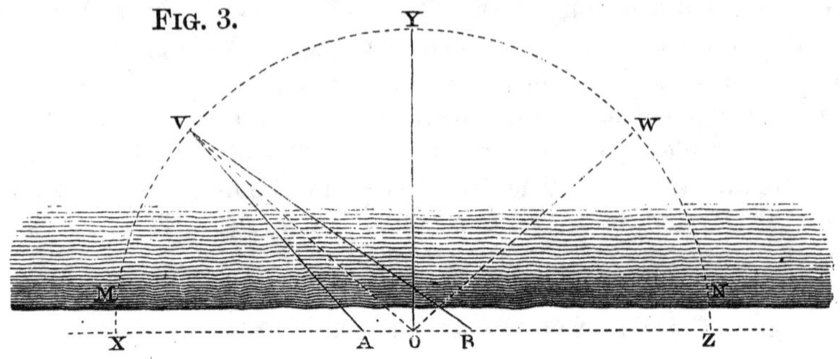

When there is no objection, we usually give to x a higher value than these relations indicate. Thus, for the light-house of the first-order at the mouth of the Canche, $p = 37{,}000m.$, a cannot have a valuation greater than 45°, we find, according to the formula, $x = 228{,}31m.$, and the intervening space has been fixed at 250 meters.

The disposition of which we have just spoken admits implicitly that lights can only preserve their distinctive character in an angular space much less than 180°. Such is the condition of all of those of this description which have been established on the coasts of France. It allows the same elevation to be given to each of the lights belonging to the same group or station, and it is easy to see that there is a double advantage in this regard; there is economy in the expense of construction, for two heights would require to be separately regulated to suit the required range, besides, two lights of different elevations are liable to be differently affected by fog, and the navigator might then believe that one of them was much farther off than the other, and deceive himself in regard to the character of the illumination.

But, if the group of lights ought to be seen in a horizon of 180° and beyond, it will become necessary to construct the light-houses of different heights, and to place them in another direction, so that the lower may never be screened or obscured by the other. The line which joins them ought to divide the space to be illuminated into about equal parts, and the difference in height should be determined theoretically, according to the condition that the two lights should not be seen from any of the points where they should appear distinct, under a less angle than 8′ if they are small lights, and of 15′ if they are light-houses. But it is easy to judge that, on account of their great range, it is almost impossible to satisfy this last condition when applied to apparatus of the two larger orders. Even if we admit that the lights would appear sufficiently distinct under an angle of 12′, a difference of 100 meters in the heights would not prevent confusion beyond a distance of about 15 miles.

The problem is hardly ever susceptible of a practical solution when the angle a approaches 90°, or goes beyond that term; the lights then blend into one, in a part more or less extended of the maritime horizon.

RANGE LIGHTS.

There are many range lights on our channel and ocean coasts, where there are numerous narrow passages. There is a small number only in the Mediterranean.

The power of these lights varies with the local circumstances. The light at Fatouville, which has already been spoken of, is of the first order, and is associated with a light of the third order upon the pier of the hospital at Honfleur, to guide navigators clear of the Ratier

Bank, which is distant nearly ten miles. The entrance to the harbor of Brest is marked by the lights of Portzic and of Petit-Minou, the one of the second and the other of the third order. The range line of the main channel of the mouth of the Loire is marked by two lights of the third order, the Commerce and the Aiguillon. But almost everywhere else lights of the fourth order are called into requisition for this kind of service, for the reason that the distance at which they are required to be seen does not exceed their range.

Many experiments have been made with the purpose of determining the minimum of the angle which two lights seen one above the other should make in a horizontal projection, so that it may be judged immediately that they are not placed upon one and the same vertical. The question is no longer one of physics; it rests upon observations of another order, and great anomalies were expected in the results. But they have been generally very few; the agreement has even been remarkable, and allows us to treat the subject with a precision of which it did not appear to be susceptible. We will limit ourselves to the citation of one of these experiments. The lights were from small apparatus of mould-glass, whose intensities were estimated to be equal to six carcel burners. The vertical distance which separated them could be varied, and the lower light was movable on a horizontal rail perpendicular to the line joining the upper light to the station of observation. This station was 772 meters distant from the lights. The observers were three in number, and after having placed the lower light on the same vertical line with the other, it was moved 10 centimeters at a time, until it was so clearly shown to be out of that line that there could be no possible indecision, even among persons little versed in such matters. The table which follows shows the facts observed:

VERTICAL DISTANCE.		HORIZONTAL DIVERSION.		Angle with the vertical of the line joining the lights.
Linear.	Angular.	Linear.	Angular.	
m.	′ ″	m.	′ ″	° ′
2.00	8.54	1.00	4.27	26.34
3.00	13.22	1.50	6.41	26.34
4.00	17.49	1.80	8.1	24.14
6.00	26.43	2.40	10.41	21.48
8.00	35.37	2.60	11.35	18.0
10.00	44.32	3.30	14.42	18.16
12.00	53.26	3.60	16.2	16.42

It is seen that the separation measured in horizontal projection increases in proportion as the vertical distance is greater, but that, nevertheless, the angle formed with the vertical by the line joining the two lights diminishes at the same time.

The results deduced from the observations may be represented by a graphic construction, which will show their agreement with sufficient clearness always, excepting in two points, those which correspond to the vertical angular distances 13′ 22″ and 35′ 37″, which evidently point out errors of observation.

In taking for ordinates the vertical angular distances, and for abscissæ the horizontal angular distances, we obtain a series of points belonging to a regular curve, leaving out of account the two anomalies of which we have just spoken, which, however, are not very marked.

FIG. 4.

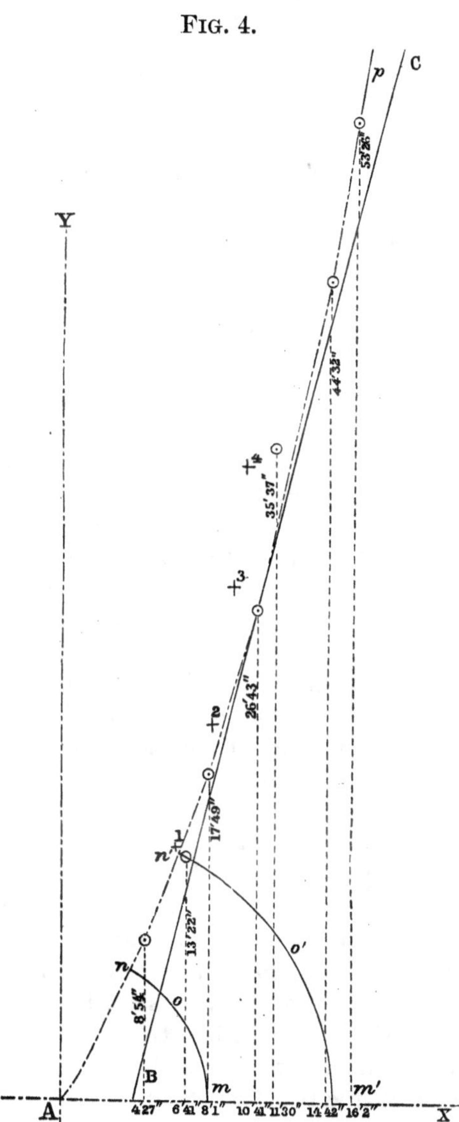

The lower light being placed at A, the origin of the cöordinates, the successive positions of the upper light may be represented in the limits of the observation by an arc of a parabola of the third degree, A n p, which will have for equation $y = 1.88\,x + 0.0054\,x^3$.

But it is to be remarked, that two lights would blend near the origin, and that that curve ought not to be admitted, except at a distance of 8′ from the point A, if the lights are of weak or little intensity, and of 15′ if we consider lights of the three larger orders, these angles being those which are regarded as the smallest under which the lights are well defined, as has been previously said. The geometrical place for the position of the upper light is then determined by the arc of the parabola n p and by the arc of the circle $n\ o\ m$, in the first case, and by the curve $n'\ p$ and the arc $n'\ o'\ m'$, in the second.

The calculation of the value of x appears rather long for practical operations, and it has been thought best to substitute for the parabola a right line, which approaches very near the middle part, and has for equation

$$y = 4\ (x - 4'.)$$

This light passes through one of the points of observation, and leaves all the others nearer to the vertical. The solutions which it gives are, then, more favorable to the interests of navigators than those of the parabola. It is indicated upon the figure by the letters B C.

The points marked 1, 2, 3, and 4 upon the same figure belong to a series of observations made with parabolic reflectors. The curve which may be deduced from it supposes a little more of correctness in the view taken by the observer than the preceding one admits of; that last is that which exacts the most angular space between the two lights.

It is much better that the heights of two lights for a range be regulated in such a manner so that the one farthest off is never exposed to the risk of being masked to the eyes of the navigator by the construction which supports the other. But it is not always possible to fulfil that condition, and it is then essential that the limits of occultation should be sufficiently distant from those of the channel that one may be assured of being in good water even when one light only is seen, and that there is time to return when the second is clearly shown.

If the passage is very contracted, a moment of inattention, an accidental occultation of the more distant light, or a momentary extinction, might cause serious consequences, and it would be prudent not to light a passage in a case where it will be impossible to place the lights in such a position that they would be always simultaneously in sight.

We proceed by way of false position in the studies relative to the sites to be assigned to two lights to serve as a range. The site A of the lower light is usually determined by local circumstances, and to the higher one is assigned the position which at first appears most suitable.

Examination is then made to ascertain if this last-named light cannot, without entailing too great expense, be established at such an elevation above the other that it may be seen through the entire length of the channel or passage. If this cannot be arranged, and if no other point appears to fulfil that condition, care is then taken that the angle of occultation m B n shall not exceed the wished for limits. Finally, it is sought to ascertain whether, at each of the points where the navigator ought to avoid a danger, a value will be found for x, (that is to say, for the angle which the two lights will make in hori-

FIG. 5.

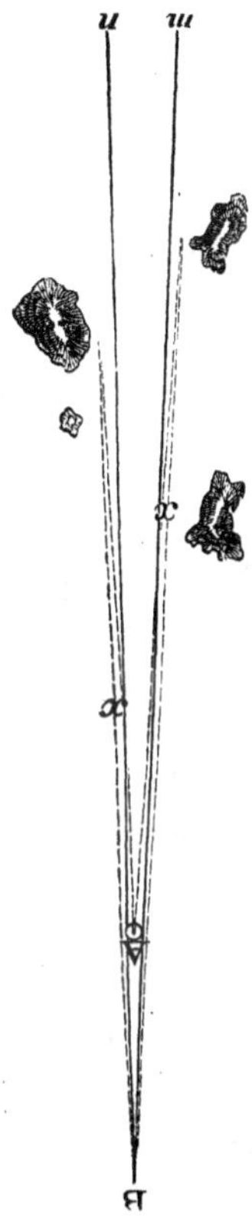

zontal projection,) at least equal to that which is deduced from the formula

$$y = 4\,(x - 4',)$$

without the real angle ever being inferior to 8′ or 15′, according to the intensities.

The same characteristic distinction may be assigned to both of the lights, when their heights are such that the most distant one will be seen above the other throughout the entire length of the channel to be lighted. But when that is not so, it will be proper to have their appearances different, as has already been said, so that the navigator may discover at once in what direction he should steer to place himself upon the line to follow. A fixed light may be associated with a fixed light varied by flashes, or a fixed white with a fixed red light, and the upper or higher light should have morepower, in proportion as it is separated from the other by a greater distance. In such cases, long eclipse lights are not employed, for the reason that both lights should always be in sight in the channel, or at least that one of them should disappear only at rare and short intervals.

The two range lights for the channel of the Sables-d'Olonne, for example, are both fixed white, because that of Chaume is seen above the other throughout the whole extent of the channel. The lights of St. George and of the sand hills of Suzac, which beacon the entrance to the Gironde, are in an analogous position, and are both fixed, but they have been colored red to distinguish them from the numerous light-houses lighted in the same navigable waters. The entrance to the port of Brest is lighted by the fixed white light of the Petit-Minou (third order) and by the light varied by flashes on the point of Portzic, (second order,) and that distinction in the characters and in the ranges has been judged necessary, for the reason that the latter appears below the other when they are seen at a short distance, and is separated from it by a space of 6,400 meters.

It frequently happens that it is only necessary to illuminate a very small arc by one light. The navigator then has but a single light in sight in the greater portion of the sea horizon, but it makes known to him, before he approaches the channel, the course which he should steer to enable him to see the second one before encountering dangers.

This circumstance is availed of to diversify the distinctive characteristics or the ranges without an unnecessary augmentation of expense.

When the distance at which the lights ought to be seen does not exceed a few miles, a small catadioptric apparatus of the fourth order is used to illuminate the entire horizon, and a parabolic reflector of 0.29*m.* of opening for the one required to light the small arc. When one of the two ought to be colored, it is to the latter that the application is made, because, more intense than the former, without requiring to be of greater range, it may be deprived of a part of its brilliancy without inconvenience. The value of the first varies from nine to eighteen burners, and that of the latter is reduced by the color to about the same rate. If the distance which separates the lights is considerable, and if, as often happens, the catoptric apparatus is the farthest from the channel, it will be necessary either to have recourse to a longer reflector, so as to augment the brilliancy by a greater concentration of the luminous rays, to place two or three in juxtaposition, or, finally, to employ the lens apparatus of the character of those represented in the figures 7, 8, 9, and 10 of Plate 12.

Thus, the light-house of Pontaillac, which, in conjunction with that of Terre Nègre, distant two miles, marks one of the passes at the mouth of the Gironde, is alternately red and white, and is lighted with three reflectors when red, and by two when white is used. It only illuminates an arc of about twelve degrees.

It is seen that the solution of the question of lighting a determined direction depends essentially upon local circumstances, and each particular case should be thoroughly studied. It is above all important never to forget that an alignment is so much the more precise as the lights are the more distant, and that the limits heretofore laid down should not be reached unless in case of absolute necessity. All of our range lights are greatly within the limits, as it is easy to see by an inspection of the charts.

CHAPTER II.

ILLUMINATING APPARATUS.

The illuminating apparatus of a light-house is essentially composed of two distinct parts:

1st. The luminous focus.

2d. The optical system designed to direct to the maritime horizon the rays of light which would diverge to the heavens, towards the earth, or to the foot of the tower.

The apparatus in actual use are illuminated by lamps, and colza oil is the combustible generally employed in them. They are divided into *catoptric apparatus* or *by reflectors*, and *dioptric apparatus* or *by lenses.* Both can be so arranged as to show colored lights.

We will examine, first, what are the considerations which govern the general arrangements of these apparatus and their accessories, after which we will describe the apparatus in most general use in the light-house service. We will conclude with a study of the different modes of producing light.

I.—CATOPTRIC APPARATUS.

Catoptric apparatus do not appear to have been applied to the illumination of light-houses before towards the close of the last century. They existed at that time upon a number of points on our seacoast, and, among others, on Cape Ailly, La Héve, on the isles of Ré and Oleron, and upon the tower of Cordouan. This latter dates 1782, and although it had no less than eighty lamps, each with a reflector, they produced so bad a light that navigators asked earnestly for a return to the preceding system, which consisted of a light produced by coal, which had been substituted for wood within a few years. The apparatus, it is true, was very defective; the lamps, supplied with flat wicks, produced but little light and much smoke, and the reflectors, in the form of spherical segments, received but a small part of the luminous rays, and did not transmit them in the direction necessary to render them most useful.

The chief engineer of the province, M. Teulère, who owed his distinction, at a later period, for increasing the height of this same tower of Cordouan, was charged with the examination of the question and the study of the means by which to remedy the evil complained of. This resulted in the production of a very remarkable Memoir, dated

26th of May, 1783, in which he exposed the inefficiency of the system with great clearness, and pointed out the principle which gave value to the catoptric apparatus. He suggested that each reflector should be parabolic in shape; that they should be illuminated by a double current of air lamp placed in the focus of the paraboloid; to place a number of reflectors in the same plane; and, finally, to give to the apparatus a movement of rotation around a vertical axis, in a way to show in succession upon all the points of the horizon the luminous beam emanating from the reflectors. This constituted in this way the eclipse lights.*

But it was not at Cordouan that the new system was first applied. It had already been experimented with successfully at other points of our seacoast, when, in 1790, the largest catoptric apparatus which had been constructed up to that date was placed upon the summit of the tower which Teulère had completed. This apparatus consisted of three groups, each of which was formed of four reflectors, ranged above each other in the same plane. These groups, separated by spaces of 120°, so as to divide the circumference into three equal parts, being supported upon a frame in the form of a triangular prism, to which a pendulum-movement machine gave rotation. The flashes succeeded each other every two minutes. The reflectors had thirty inches (0.812*m.*) of open-

* Borda has the credit, generally, of being the inventor of parabolic reflectors and eclipse lights, and Argand of double current-of-air lamps.

But, it was in 1784, after having heard of the Memoir of Teulère from Marshal Broglie, then Minister of Marine, that the learned academican caused to be executed for the port of Dieppe, and without claiming the merit of others, a small revolving apparatus, consisting of five parabolic reflectors. The application of the new system to the tower of Cordouan was probably delayed, for the reason that the question at that time was the raising of the tower. The project of that important work was presented in 1786, and was immediately commenced. Borda charged himself then to make the apparatus conceived by Teulère, who could not find at Bordeaux a sufficiently expert artist to do it.

As to the inventor of the double current-of-air lamp, it is to be remarked that the authors who attributed it to Argand only go back to 1784 or 1786, while the Memoir of Teulère bears date 1783. Besides, that engineer, who is named as the inventor of the parabolic reflectors, does not insist upon that which relates to the burner of the lamp. He contents himself with saying that Argand had the same idea that he had, and took a prominent part in regard to it.

Without doubt, the title of Teulère to an absolute priority may be contested. It would be very strange if no one before him had thought of utilizing, for the transmission of light, the property best known of the parabola; and it appeared that a small revolving apparatus, of three reflectors, (probably spherical shells,) had been placed at the entrance to the port of Marstrand, in Sweden, prior to 1783. But the French engineer invented it himself, and had the merit to conceive a complete and rational system in all its parts. He has been the real inventor of catoptric lights, in this sense that they are very defective under all the aspects in which the question has been viewed, and that there has been nothing essential found to add to his conception. Except the proportions and some few details of construction, the actual catoptric apparatus, the most used, are in entire conformity to those of Teulère.

ing. Illuminated at first by lamps, the dimensions of whose burners were too restricted, they gave little divergence; the flash was very quick, but it only continued during five seconds. In 1793, the diameters of the burners were augmented, and the duration of the flashes reached then to ten seconds.

About the same time, Teulère fitted in the light-house of Chaume, at the Sables d'Olonne, an apparatus composed of only three reflectors, in the focus of each of which was a burner of 0.033*m.* diameter.

This mode of illumination constituted a considerable progress, and had a marked success. The greater part of the maritime nations adopted it with eagerness, and until within a recent period it has been exclusively used on the coasts of England, as well as by the most of maritime powers of the north of Europe.

CATOPTRIC APPARATUS ACTUALLY IN USE.

The catoptric apparatus most in actual use in the light-house service of France is composed of one or several parabolic reflectors, each one illuminated by a double current-of-air lamp, fed by colza oil. These reflectors are of two kinds: One kind, which is often designated by the name of *photophores*, (concave mirrors,) having but one piece, and is formed by the revolution of an arc of a parabola around its own axis, as with those of Teulère; the others are in two pieces, whose surfaces are formed by the revolution of a parabola around the vertical axis passing through its focus. These last were invented by Bordier Marcet, and named by him *sideral apparatus.* The Figures 11, 12, and 13 of Plate 12 represent a photophore mounted upon its stands, and the Figures 14 and 15 of the same plate show a sideral apparatus enclosed in a portable lantern.

PARABOLIC REFLECTORS OF ONE PIECE.

It is easy to see, from an inspection of the figure below, that the photophore concentrates into one single luminous beam the greater part of the rays emitted from the focus (O) of the paraboloid, all those which are comprised in the angle O A P B except the losses due to the absorption by the metallic surface and to the occultation produced by the burner of the lamp. The rays emitted directly from the focus, and included in the angle A O B diverge and form a luminous cone, the upper half of which is without useful effect for illumination. If the luminous focus be reduced to a point, all the reflected rays will be parallel to the axis, and the transverse section of the combined beams of light will be at all points precisely equalto the opening of the photophore, but such is not the case; the dimensions of the illuminating body are marked relatively to those of the reflector, and each point of the surface reflects a conical beam, whose divergence is as much greater

FIG. 6.

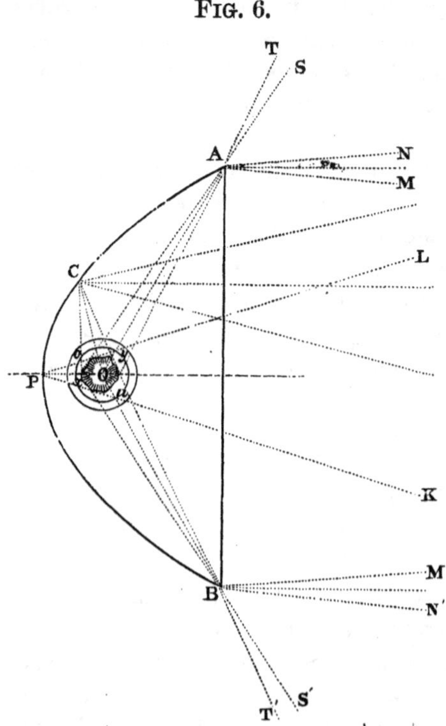

as the reflecting point is nearer to the focus, and the flame is more expanded. The beams which come from the reflector are not then cylindrical, but conical. Besides, the luminous rays are not equally distributed, in the entire extent of the cone, which it will be easy to see by observing the direction which they take after having been reflected.

Let *u x y z*, Figure 6, be the horizontal section of the flame; the most divergent rays in the horizontal plane, are those which tangents to that circumference come in contact with the reflector at its summit P, and the angle L P K represents the horizontal divergence of the apparatus. The extreme rays, such as *z* A, *u* A, are reflected following the lines A M, A N, which form with the axis of the angles equals between them, and with the angles *z* A O, O A *u*. The angle of divergence of these luminous rays is equal to M A N. We may determine, in the same manner, the value of the divergence produced by any point whatever, as C of the reflector. That divergence is precisely equal to the angle which subtends the tangents coming from that point to the circumference of the flame. In the horizontal plane, on that side of the point where the lines A N, B N′ come in contact with the lines P L and P K, the angular space L P K embraces all the reflected rays. To the right and to the left is an angular space comprised between the lines L P and S *z*, or K P and S′ *z*, in which we see the rays coming direct from the focus; lastly, in the angles S A T, S′ B T,′ we find but a part of these rays, which diminish at leaving these lines A S, B S,′ and disappear at A T and B T.′

We may see, in the same way, the course which the luminous rays take in any plane whatever.

Let us take, for an example, the vertical plane. Let A P B, Figure 7, the section of the reflector *x y z u*, be that of the flame, and O the focus of the paraboloid, the ray *z* M, coming from the point *z*, normally to the parabola, mark the limit of the divergence of reflected rays below the horizontal plane, and the normal *u* N, coming from the point *u*, is that of the divergence above the same plane. Any point

C of the upper part of the reflector brings below the horizon all the rays coming from the flame to the right of the line O C, and reflects above that plane all the rays coming from the other side. The former are comprised in the angle L C K = O C *z*, and the latter in the angle L′ C K = O C *x*. The inverse effect is produced by all the points of the parabola which are situated below the focus.

FIG 7.

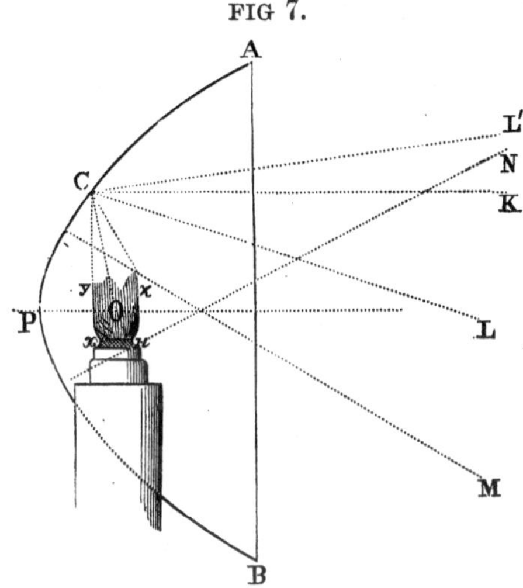

The divergence which operates in the horizontal plane and below it is useful to the illumination, for, if it diminishes the luminous intensity, it has the effect of expanding the light upon a greater surface, and there is nothing to regret. But it is not the same with the rays sent above the horizon, as they are lost. Besides, that which is of more importance still than to draw part of all the reflected rays, is to illuminate to the greatest possible distance, to direct the most intense luminous beam tangentially to the horizon, and that is accomplished by placing the flame at such a height that the most brilliant part of it will be in the focus of the paraboloid. That disposition has above all the merit of transmitting more of the rays below than above the horizontal plane.

When the apparatus is greatly elevated above the level of the sea, it is so inclined that its prolonged axis will be tangent to the horizon; but, in most cases, the height is not such as to render it necessary to resort to that measure, for the tangent to the horizon is sensibly horizontal.

The reflectors of one piece, which still now constitute some of our illuminating apparatus, are of three sizes. Those belonging to the old light-houses, received since the invention of the lens system, are habitually called *reflectors of Lenoir*, the name of the maker. They have an opening of 0.85*m*., with a depth of 0.345*m*., and their focus is situated at 0.131*m*. from the summit. They are always lighted by lamps whose burners have a diameter of 0.024*m*., which consume about 60 grammes of colza oil per hour, and whose intensity is equivalent to 1.60 of carcel burner. Recourse is had to lamps with two concentric wicks, when circumstances render it necessary to have at the same time greater brilliancy and greater divergence. The burners of those last lamps have a diameter of 0.039*m*., their consumption reaches to 175 grammes of colza oil per hour, and their intensity may be estimated as high as five carcel burners. The divergence of the reflected rays in the horizontal plane is equal to about 12,° when the lamp has a single wick, and to 18° when it has two wicks.

Other parabolic reflectors of one piece have an opening of 0.50*m.*, a depth of 0.195*m.*, a focal distance of 0.08*m.*, and are illuminated by lamps with one wick of 0.024*m.* diameter. They have a divergence in the horizontal plane of about 20°.

The reflectors now in most common use have only an opening of 0.29*m.*, and a depth of 0.125*m.* Their focus is situated at 0.042*m.* from the summit. They are for the most part illuminated by lamps with one wick, of 0.021*m.* diameter, consuming 50 grammes of colza oil per hour, and in intensity estimated at 1.30 of carcel burner. Inferior to the preceding ones in relative useful effect, they are, on the other hand, lighter, more easily placed, and less expensive. Their divergence in the horizontal plane is about 36°.

DISTRIBUTION OF THE LUMINOUS RAYS.

The following table exhibits the distribution of the luminous rays by different apparatus in the horizontal plane. The numbers therein inserted have been adopted by the light-house service as representing sufficiently near that which has been found in practice. They are deduced from numerous experiments, which have not been without anomalies, which may be readily conceived on account of the irregularities in the focus, of which the reflectors are rarely exempt. The *maxima* which have been found in these essays have been reduced to about $\frac{1}{5}$, in taking into account the imperfections of the service, and the absorption of the luminous rays by the plate glass of the lanterns.

Degrees of Latitude.	Intensities, by Carcel Burners, of Parabolic Reflectors.			
	Of 0.85*m.*, with lamp of 5 burners.	Of 0.85*m.*, with lamp of 1.60*b.*	Of 0.50*m.*, with lamp of 1.60*b.*	Of 0.29*m.*, with lamp of 1.30*b.*
0	760	550	200	60
1	752	540	196	60
2	715	470	185	59
3	640	315	166	57
4	515	150	140	54
5	360	40	110	50
6	220	5	75	44
7	100	....	46	37
8	30	....	25	30
9	5	....	10	22
10	....	....	4	16
11	....	....	....	12
12	....	....	....	9
13	....	....	....	7
14	....	....	....	5
15	....	....	....	4
16	....	....	....	3
17	....	....	....	2.5
18	....	....	....	2

The brilliancy in the axis, and the divergence in the horizontal plane of a reflector of 0.85*m.*, illuminated by a double-wick lamp, consuming 110 grammes of colza oil per hour, and presenting an intensity of 3 burners, may be valued, respectively, at 580 burners and of 16°.

ADVANTAGES OF PARABOLIC REFLECTORS.

FIG. 8.

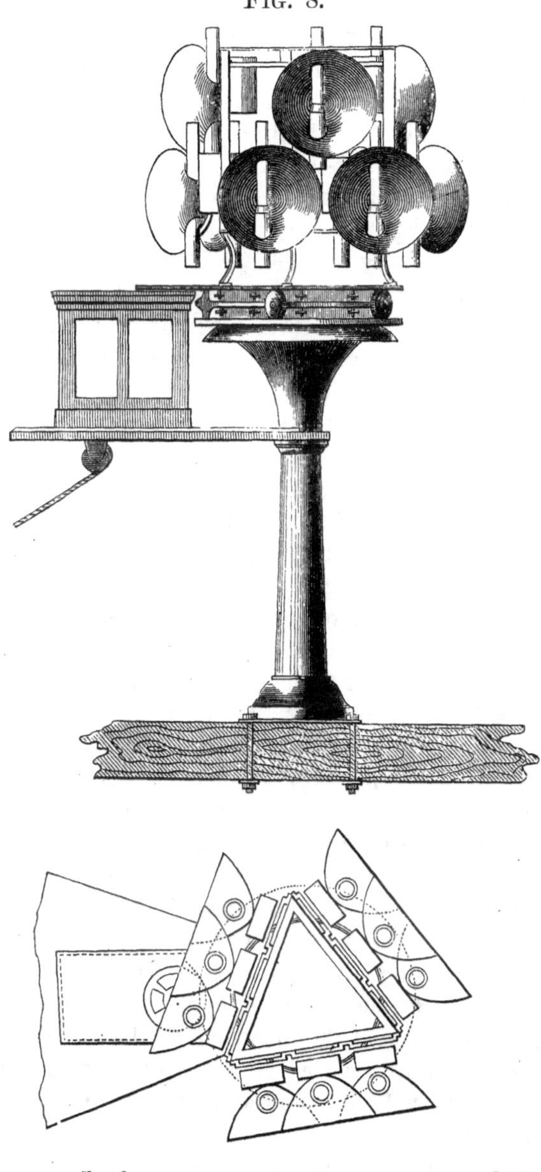

Parabolic reflectors possess the advantage of being lighter and less expensive than lens apparatus. They suit well, and are frequently used under the following circumstances:

1. For the illumination of narrow passages, or to form one of the range lights of a channel.

2. To strengthen, in a fixed direction, a light whose range is sufficient for other parts of the sea horizon. It is for this purpose that a small parabolic reflector has been placed in the lantern of the light-house at Terre Nègre to increase the intensity of the light in the direction of the North Pass of the mouth of the Gironde.

3. For illuminating floating lights, which, however, may, without doubt, admit the use of lens apparatus, but for which they are not so well suited as they are for fixed structures.

4. For the apparatus of temporary lights.

The apparatus represented above, Fig. 8, in plan and elevation, is such a one. It is seen composed of nine reflectors in three faces of an equilateral triangle. A small revolving machine gives it motion, and causes eclipses, more or less frequent, according to the rapidity of its motion. The range of this light is about 15 miles.

Fig. 9.

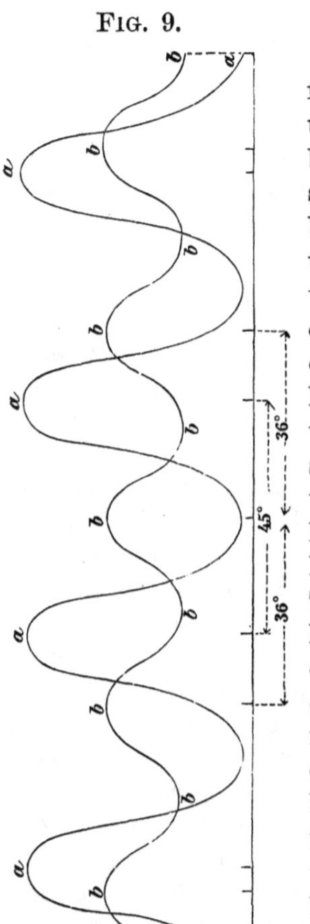

Parabolic reflectors are better suited to the forming of eclipse than for fixed lights until the whole or greater part of the horizon is to be illuminated. In the first case, it allows the successive transmission of the same luminous beam to every point of the horizon, and with the same range in every direction; whilst it will be necessary to greatly multiply them to obtain a uniform distribution of the light in every part of the zone to be lighted. This last point, however, is of little importance when the illumination of a pass is under consideration, because there is almost always advantage in directing the greater part of the luminous rays along the axis of the channel. But it is not so under ordinary circumstances. Thus, the illuminating apparatus for fixed lights on board of light-vessels, and such is the character of the most of those lights, are required to illuminate the entire horizon, and are formed by a series of reflectors (photophores) of 0.29*m*. of opening, arranged in a circle in a lantern, with a mast in the centre, around which it hoists. The first apparatus of this description, which was made in France, consisted, like those of England, of only eight reflectors, (photophores,) equally distant from each other, and it resulted that the observer perceived a very brilliant light when it was placed in the axis of one of the reflectors, and he only saw the light coming direct from the two focii in environs of the bisection of the angle formed by the axes of the two contiguous reflectors. To an angular space of 36°, in which the luminous intensity may range from 60 burners to 2, succeeded an angular space of 9°, in which the light was uniformly distributed, and reached no greater power than of two burners.

The curve *a a a*, of the Figure 9 above, shows the distribution of the light emanating from one of these apparatus in the extent of a semicircle.

It has been constructed, in taking the angular spaces for abscissæ, to a scale of 0.01*m.* for 15°, and the luminous intensities for ordinates to a scale of 0.01*m.* for 20 burners.

A more equal illumination will be obtained by increasing the number of reflectors, because then the curves of two contiguous reflectors cross each other. With 24 reflectors, the luminous intensity will not vary more than from 67 to 68 burners from one point to another, which may be considered as a uniform distribution. The intensities will not differ out of proportion if but 16 reflectors are used. Their maximum will be 60 burners, and their minimum about 25 burners.

But such a large number of reflectors make it necessary to give to the lantern dimensions which militate against the special conditions which belong to floating lights, and will, besides, conduce to a consumption of oil far beyond those of the ordinary lights of the same range.

The apparatus for floating fixed lights, recently established at different points on our coast, have been so arranged that they consist of 10 reflectors, (photophores,) each illuminated by a lamp of one wick of 0*m.*021 diameter, consuming 50 grammes of oil per hour, and in which the flame has been placed, but at 0.01*m.* nearer to the summit of the parabola, so as to give a greater divergence. The curve *b b b*, of the figure 9, shows how one of these apparatus distributes the light in the horizontal plane. The decentralization produces a marked reduction of intensity in the axis of the reflector. The most brilliant parts do not attain a greater intensity than of 38 burners; but the minimum of intensity does not descend below 18, and it suffices for a range for the height of these lights above the level of the sea. The plate 13 represents an apparatus of this description.

The divergence of these apparatus in the vertical sense is at the same time more marked than if the flame were in the focus of the paraboloid; but it has the merit of preventing the occultations which the motion of the vessel tends to produce. The luminous rays which are uselessly thrown up towards the sky when in a state of repose are sometimes usefully brought to the sea by the motion of the reflectors caused by the sea, which are not placed always immediately in the vertical plane, notwithstanding the system of suspension employed.

Lens apparatus might be substituted for parabolic reflectors and thus realize an economy in the combustible. But that advantage has not appeared sufficiently great to counteract the inherent inconvenience of the system, and the studies which were commenced in that direction have not been followed up.

In revolving apparatus for floating lights, the reflectors are to the number of eight or more, and they are sometimes so arranged in groups as to produce very brilliant flashes. The apparatus recently constructed for one of the light-vessels off Dunkerque, is composed of eight reflectors of 0.37*m.* of opening, 0.185*m.* of depth, and 0.047*m.* focal distance, the flames of which are not uncentred. It is represented on plate 14.

If it be desired to employ reflectors for the illumination of a light-house for a fixed light to be established under ordinary circumstances, and to illuminate far off and an extended horizon, it will be necessary not only to take care to place the burner out of the focus, as in the case of the fixed lights for light-vessels, but also to employ through choice the large reflectors similar to those of Lenoir, so as to reduce the divergence in the vertical plane as much as apparatus of this sort will allow.

It is useless to enter into the examination of the dispositions which it might be convenient to adopt for that purpose, for they vary according to given circumstances, and are, besides, easily imagined. Not a single apparatus of that kind is now in actual use on the coast of France; those which existed heretofore have all been replaced by lens apparatus, in the double interest of navigation and of the public treasury.

There are cases in which circumstances will render the employment of these large reflectors useful; such as has been previously stated, when it becomes necessary to illuminate a long passage or channel having an angular space of 12° to 15°. The light at Pontaillac, for example, had to fulfil that office, and it was necessary, besides, to give it a character which would prevent its being mistaken for other lights at the mouth of the Gironde. It is fitted with three reflectors of 0*m.*85, directed to the axis of the channel. Two of them are each illuminated by a single-wick lamp, and the third by a double-concentric-wick lamp with a red chimney. A revolving machine gives a motion which alternates a screen which masks the colored reflector light, then uncovering it, and places a red pane of glass before the two others. That revolution is rapid, and changes at regular intervals of 20 seconds, so that the light appears alternately red and white during that interval of time, without interposed eclipses. There was some thought of having the red-light reflector revolve, instead of masking it for the purpose of utilizing in a particular direction the rays which are actually lost during the entire appearance of the white light; but the local circumstances did not seem to warrant the expense which such a disposition of the apparatus would necessitate.

SIDERAL APPARATUS.

In the sideral apparatus, the luminous rays are distributed uniformly to every part of the sea horizon, with the exception of those which the lateral reflectors send back, which will be spoken of hereafter. If the luminous focus were reduced to a point, the only lost rays—allowance being made for the absorption of the reflecting surface—would be, as shown by the figure below, those which are situated in the space comprised between the horizontal plane passing through the focus of the paraboloid, and the conical surface generated by the rotation of the line O M around the vertical axis O P. But, as in the reflectors of a single piece, the loss is much greater in proportion to the dimensions of the illuminating body. It is easy to determine it by following the graphic illustration which has been submitted above, and it therefore appears unnecessary to pursue the subject further.

FIG. 10.

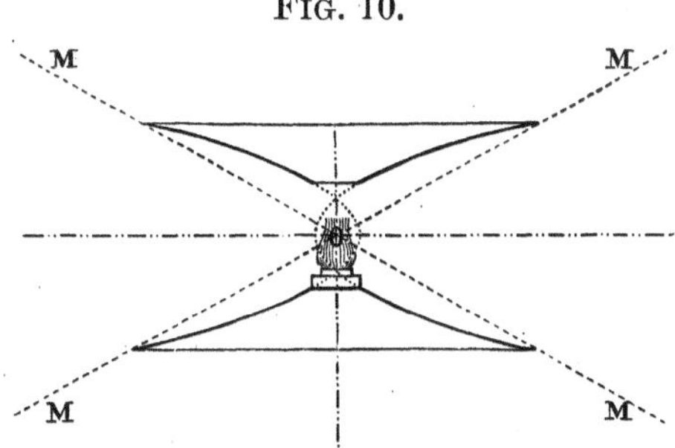

Whenever a sideral apparatus is not required to illuminate the entire horizon, and that is habitually the case, the reservoir of the lamp is placed in the dark or, dead angle, and on each side of it parabolic reflectors, which unite with the two pieces of the apparatus, and return to usefulness the luminous rays which diverge from the land side.

These apparatus are of but very limited dimensions, and produce lights having only a short range. Their brilliancy does not exceed about 3½ burners.

They are always placed in small movable lanterns which hoist upon a wooden scaffolding, or upon a chandelier between two directing posts.

Sideral apparatus recommended themselves heretofore by their lightness and small price, and they have been used to a certain extent in illuminating our coasts. But the small dioptric apparatus of mould or polished glass, which will be noticed hereafter, are preferable to them under all circumstances, have caused them to be abandoned and the new ones substituted for them.

MODE OF CONSTRUCTING AND ATTENDING UPON REFLECTORS.

All the reflectors are made from sheets of copper, plated with silver, which are shaped upon a matrix.

It is their defect that they lose a great deal of their reflecting power when their polish has been changed, or when they are not kept perfectly clean. It is not necessary that either one of these defects should be very marked to reduce the quantity of the light emanating from the apparatus.

I.—DIOPTRIC APPARATUS.

The property possessed by convex lenses, of refracting nearly parallel to their axes, all the rays emanating from a focal point, called them to fulfil an office analogous to that of the parabolic reflectors; but they could not be applied to the illumination of light-houses in preserving the continuous spherical form which belongs to them. Constructed necessarily upon larger dimensions, they would have been very thick at the centre; and thence three grave difficulties: considerable absorption of the luminous rays by the lens; deviations more or less numerous in consequence of air bubbles, of striæ or of differences of density in the mass of glass; and of such weight as to render it very difficult to arrive at a proper disposition of the apparatus.

LENSES IN ECHELON.

Buffon saw dimly the solution; without dreaming, for other reasons, of maritime illumination, he had proposed to set up the lenses by echelons. But he supposed that they would be formed of a single piece, and did not discover the means which he might have drawn from that arrangement to direct the luminous rays in the most satisfactory manner. The invention was neither practical nor complete, and it was forgotten for a long time, when, in 1819, a young engineer of the Corps of Bridges and Roads, already a celebrated natural philosopher, was attached to the light-house service. (Commission des Phares.) Like Buffon, and without doubting that the idea was new, Augustin Fresnel conceived the echelon lenses, but he did not rest there; he immediately judged that that form ought to conduce to correct the spherical aberration, a defect so much graver as the lenses increase in dimensions; he recognized all the applications of which the new system was susceptible, and he resolved upon the means of execution, leaving to a not distant future the care of perfecting them.

His lenses were composed of a central part and of successive echelons, cast and worked separately, and afterwards solidly joined together.

Their profile was formed, on one side, by a right line, so as to facilitate the execution, and the centres, such as the radii and the amplitudes of the arcs of circle of the opposite face, were calculated upon the condition to reduce as much as possible the spherical aberration and the thickness of the glass.

DISPOSITION OF THE LENSES.

The profile adopted, two systems of lenses naturally flow from it:

1st. In giving to it a movement of rotation around the horizontal axis passing through the focal point, a lens of annular elements is obtained, possessing the property of reuniting in one bundle or beam of parallel rays all the luminous rays emanating from the focus, in the same manner as by parabolic reflectors. As several of these lenses are placed so as to form a prism to a polygonal basis, having for axis the vertical passing through their focii, but one source of light occupies that point, and which is made to turn around the axis of the lenticular drum thus composed; the luminous beams emanating from the lenses being brought successively to all points of the horizon, and none of the light being seen in the intervals. We shall have an eclipse light.

2d. If the same profile turns around the vertical axis passing through the focus, it will form a cylindrical surface, which has the property of distributing uniformly upon the entire horizon the luminous rays emanating from the focus which come in contact with it. That constitutes a fixed light.

LENSES OF VERTICAL ELEMENTS.

A third kind of lens, to which recourse is sometimes had, consists in transporting the profile parallel to itself in a vertical plane; this movement creates a plane lens with vertical elements, which has the property to reunite all the rays emanating from the focus in one beam comprised between two vertical planes. It is easy to judge that in placing one lens of this description in front of the rays which have already passed through a cylindrical lens, they collect them all into one beam similar to those produced by annular lenses. The first acts horizontally, and the second vertically. Although they double the number of lenses and are little favorable to the economy of light, that arrangement is sometimes employed in lights varied by flashes, as we shall see further on. The figures 1 and 3 of the plate 6 show an example of an apparatus of this description.

HEIGHT OF THE LENSES.

The height of the lenticular drum ought to be kept in a certain relation with the focal distance. There is a limit outside of which there will be loss, by the reflection upon the interior face of the lens, of a marked portion of the luminous rays, and on the other hand, the salient angles of the echelons the furthest from the centre will become so sharp that their execution will be very difficult, in the same time failing to present sufficient guarantees of durability. The angle at the focus which subtends the drum of the lens apparatus has been fixed at first at 45°, but it has been judged that it might go further with advantage, and it varies actually from 56° to 67°, according to the nature of the apparatus.

DISPOSITIONS RELATIVE TO RAYS PASSING ABOVE OR BELOW THE LENTICULAR DRUM.

The rays passing below the drum uselessly light the foot of the tower; those which are raised above it spread themselves out in the upper parts of the atmosphere, and they will be consequently all lost to maritime illumination if recourse is not had to dispositions of the proper kind to direct them to the horizon.

Different systems have been conceived by Augustin Fresnel, with the view to utilize these two parts of emitted light.

In 1822, in the first large apparatus which he had constructed, and which was placed upon the Cordouan light-house tower, eight small lenses of 0.50*m*. of focus, forming a kind of pavillion above the lamp, collected all the upper luminous rays, and sent them out in beams upon the large plane mirrors which were placed to direct them to the horizon. The apparatus was for eclipses, and its section octagonal. Its upper part revolved with the drum, but the panels of the two divisions of the system, instead of being placed upon the same axes, were deviated in such a manner that the two flashes were consecutive and not simultaneous. He could have employed the quantity of light obtained by the new dispositions to augment the intensity of the flashes. He preferred, and with good reason, to use them to prolong their duration.

The rays thrown out below the drum only form a small part of the light emanating from the focus, and Augustin Fresnel did not at first attach much importance to the means of collecting them. However, he announced, in a note placed at the end of his Memoir of 1822, that they could be directed to the horizon by means of small plates of silvered glass, fixed below the large lenses, and *arranged in a manner similar to the pieces in a window-blind*, with the proper inclination to reflect the rays in the wished-for direction. That idea was carried out in several apparatus, but the small panes of glass, being plane, only solved the problem approximately.

Some years after, they were replaced by the horizontal zones, composed of curved silvered mirrors, and zones of the same kind were substituted in the moveable part of the apparatus above the drum. Each of these zones, of which the mirrors were in juxtaposition, could be considered as generated by the revolution of an arc of a parabola, having for focus that of the apparatus, and revolving around the vertical passing through the same point.* The luminous rays collected by them were no longer devoted to the prolongation of the duration of the flashes in the revolving lights; they were distributed uniformly upon the entire sea horizon, and they constituted a fixed light, which, appearing during the eclipses, was for the purpose of allowing navigators never to lose sight of the light seen while approaching the coast; that is to say, from the moment it became of most importance to know their exact position. In the light-houses with fixed lights, these para-

*However, in cases where it was impossible to give an exact parabolic curve to the mirrors, they were ranged according to oscillating spherical surface of the fragments of paraboloid which they ought to have formed.

bolic mirrors increased the intensity of the light. The dispositions adopted above and below the drum were the same as in all the light-houses.*

That solution left something more yet to desire, although it was very happy in theory. It was necessary above all, that the mirrors should utilize the light quite as well as the lenses, at least when they were new, and their reflecting powers should only diminish in a great proportion from the time the silvering becomes worn. They are liable to become deranged in their positions by the necessary cleaning, and the keepers are not always careful to replace them properly. Finally, their construction offered such difficulties that the engineers were obliged to become very tolerant in inspecting and receiving them, and the price, though very high, was not considered sufficient by the constructors.

CATADIOPTRIC RINGS.

An entirely new and completely irreproachable arrangement was conceived by the illustrious inventor. It consisted in transmitting the rays to the horizon by the way of refraction and of total reflection by means of rings of triangular section. But the theoretical conception could not always be put into immediate execution. The fabrication of the lenses have proved it. Before obtaining them under the regular forms which gave to them the actual machines, it became necessary to give them up, and to accept in their stead the polygonal shape, and to compose them in a series of small spherical surfaces, ranged vase-fashion. Recourse could not be had to the same method for the new rings, and he was compelled for a long time to limit himself to the application of them to the small apparatus for which the work of turning did not require implements, which was considered too expensive.†

Figure 11 shows the course of a luminous ray in one of these rings. Starting from the focus F, it is refracted at A, follows the direction A B, becomes totally reflected on the surface M N, takes the direction B C, and at last leaves the ring, following the horizontal line H. C.

The profile of the catadioptric rings being given, it may, as in the case of the lenses in echelon, receive a revolving motion around the

* This system having been abandoned, we do not think it necessary to represent it upon a special plate, inasmuch as it will be found in a great many apparatus actually in use. The figures 2 of the plates 19, 20, and 24 appear to give, besides, a sufficiently correct idea of it.

† The fixed light of the Gravelines light-house was the first light of the third order which received the catadioptric rings, and its construction bears date 1842; they were applied the following year to fixed lights of the first order. It was not until 1852 that the annular catadioptric panels of the first order were, for the first time, constructed. They were executed by Mr. Henry Lepaute, placed in the light-house of Ailly, and employed to prolong the duration of the flashes.

Fig. 11.

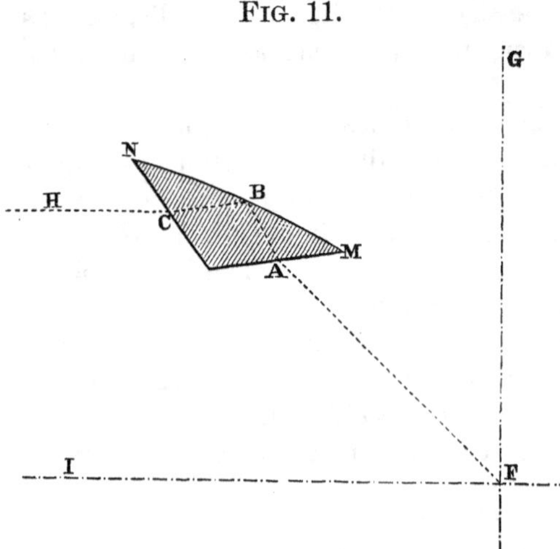

vertical axis F G, passing through the focus, or take this movement around the horizontal axis F I, leading through the same point. In the first case, it distributes the light uniformly around the entire horizón, and constitutes an element of fixed light; in the second, it reunites all the rays into one band or beam, after the manner of the lenses employed in the eclipse-light apparatus. These two applications were made during the lifetime of Augustin Fresnel, but only to the small apparatus. The first to the fixed-light apparatus of the kind represented by the figures 1, 2, 3, and 4 of the Plate 12; both at the time to the apparatus of still more limited dimensions, which were employed for sometime for the lighting of the canal of St. Martin, at Paris. The front part of these last distributed the light equally upon one-half of the circumference, after the manner of a fixed-light apparatus of 180° arc, and prolonged at each extremity by a half lens in the dioptric and catadioptric parts, which produced a luminous beam, comparatively very intense, directed normally to the meridian plane of the apparatus. Thus were found united on a small scale, and for a useful purpose, the two principal systems of panels of both kinds of profiles. This gives an almost complete summary of the valuable invention.

Fig. 12.

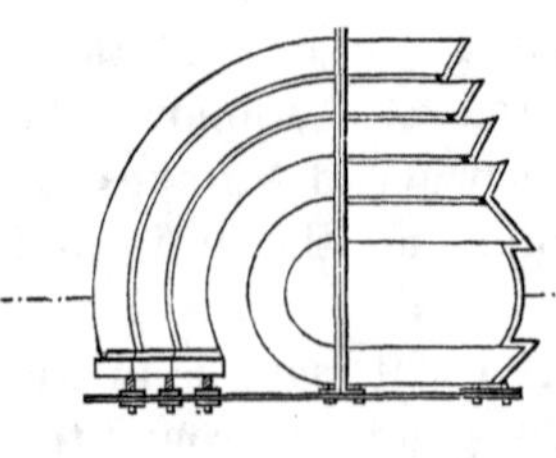

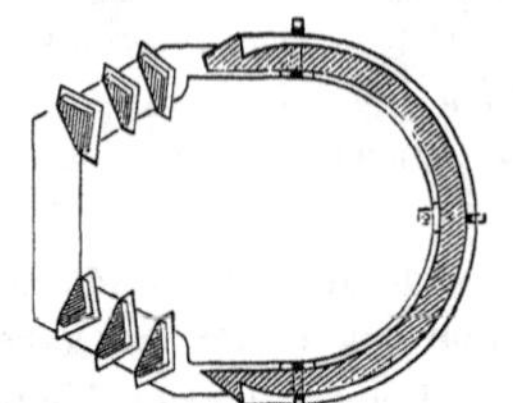

Figure 12 represents one of these apparatus, which is rigorously preserved in the Museum of the Commission of Lights, among types of the most ancient lenses. They are given in lateral elevation, and the horizontal section taken at the height of the focal plane.

The essential was established. The just praise which has been awarded to the French illuminating apparatus, the development which all the maritime powers wished to give to the illumination of their coasts with the new invention which favored it, encouraged our constructors, enabled them to erect establishments for their manufacture upon a large scale, and brought forth incessant improvements and ameliorations in their productions. Mirrors are no longer constructed, and the catadioptric rings are applied under various and different forms to the largest apparatus.

SPHERICAL REFLECTORS.

When an apparatus is not required to illuminate the entire horizon, it is important to direct to the sea the rays which would diverge uselessly from the landside. For that purpose, recourse is had to spherical reflectors, which cover the dead angle of the apparatus, and return to the focal point the rays which, leaving that point, come in contact with them. These rays, pursuing their course, strike the lenses opposite, which refract them in the same way that the others are refracted. However, it is not upon the exact focus that the reflected rays come to cross each other, it is a little higher, for the centre of the spherical reflector is fixed at a little height above that point. Two motives concur in causing the adoption of this disposition. If the centre of the spherical surfaces coincide with the focal point, a large part of the reflected rays will be arrested by the body of the lamp, and, on the other hand, the burner will be exposed to be burnt (fused) and the wicks carbonized, for the reason that they will become too much heated.

It results, therefore, that the greater part of the reflected rays are sent through the lenses, following the lines more or less inclined to the horizon, and which increase the flash or brilliancy of the light in a much greater proportion at a short than a great distance. It is seen that there would not be any economical advantage to substitute for these reflectors much more expensive apparatus, even when these last would possess the merit of absorbing less of the luminous rays, and such are those which may be obtained by means of catadioptric double reflection rings. It is not possible to make a reduction of expense in questions of that kind.

In some apparatus of the first order the reflectors have been placed on the landside, not only in the height of the drum, but, also, both above and below. That has been abandoned, for the reason that the quantity of rays uselessly brought back by the reflectors from above and below, have not been thought sufficiently great to compensate for the expense of placing them; besides, it has been found that it is not without interest for the supervision of the service to transmit a little light landward.

These reflectors are always made in sheets of copper plated with silver. One of our constructors, Mr. L. Sautter, makes them of glass, silverplated on the exterior surface. A much better polish is thus obtained, while the attendance upon them is much easier; but, perhaps, the shape is not equally regular.

DIMENSIONS AND INTENSITY OF THE FLAMES.

In the catoptric apparatus the number of lamps is increased when it is necessary to have a more powerful light. In the lens apparatus it is upon the lamp itself which it is necessary to act upon, and to make it vary for that purpose the number and the diameter of the wicks. The dimensions of the apparatus regulate themselves by those of the flame.

The diameters of, and the spaces between the wicks actually in use, were determined in 1821 by Augustin Fresnel and Arago, and the long experience to which they have been subjected since that time have fully justified them. They were fixed in a way to insure regularity of the service, and to allow the utilizing of the best part of the expended combustible.

ORDERS OF THE LIGHTS.

The burners of the lamps of lights of the first order carry four concentric wicks, those of the second order three, those of the third order two, and all the apparatus illuminated by a lamp of a single wick are ranged as of the fourth order.

The Plate 15 represents these burners on a scale of one-half, as well as the flames generated by them. The burners are seen in elevation on one side, and in vertical section on the other. The plans are taken from above.

The table below shows the regulation dimensions, and the luminous intensities of the flames:

Order of light.	No. of wicks.	Dimensions of the flame fully developed.		Luminous intensity in carcel burners.	Numbers of the figures corresponding to the Plate 15.
		Maximum diameter.	Height above the burner.		
		mm.	*mm.*		
1st order	4	90	100	23	1 and 2
2d order	3	75	80	15	3 and 4
3d order, large model	2	45	70	5	5 and 6
3d order, small model		38	65	3	
4th order, large model	1	30	45	1.6	7 and 8
4th order, small model		27	37	1.3	

DIMENSIONS OF THE APPARATUS.

It is easy to see that it is necessary to observe a certain relation between the dimensions of a lens apparatus and those of the flame which illuminates it, as much to maintain within proper limits the expenses of the first fitting and establishing, as to derive the full benefit of the best part of the light produced at the focal point. A certain divergence is, in effect, necessary to insure that the entire illumination of the surface of the sea, and that the flashes of the eclipse lights have a proper duration; but if it is too marked, a notable part of the luminous rays will be lost, and the intensity of the light will be reduced in a great proportion.

These considerations have led to the regulating of the dimensions of the apparatus of the different orders, as shown by the figures of Plate 3 and the following table:

Order of the apparatus.	Interior diameter of the drum.	Height of the optical parts.			Total height, including the interior frames.	Figures corresponding to Plate 3.
		Of the lower part.	Of the drum.	Of the upper part.		
	m.	m.	m.	m.	m.	
1st order	1.840	0.539	0.980	1.001	2.590	1
2d order	1.400	0.378	0.854	0.810	2.069	2
3d order, large model	1.000	0.278	0.660	0.593	1.576	3
3d order, small model	0.500	0.144	0.300	0.258	0.722	4
4th order, large model	0.375	0.105	0.226	0.196	0.541	5
4th order, small model	0.300	0.084	0.180	0.157	0.433	6

DISTRIBUTION OF THE LUMINOUS RAYS.

Let us now examine how the luminous rays directed from the flame upon the different parts of a lens apparatus act.

The following figures represent a fragment of the plane and profile of an apparatus of the first order of eclipses, each panel of which embraces one-eighth of the circumference.

The focus of the drum which forms the dioptric lenses is situated at O on both of them. All the rays emanating from the focus, as O M, O N, are refracted parallel to that which, starting from the same point, passes through the axis of the lens; the others diverge more or less, follow the part of the flame which sends; and the extreme limits of the divergence, in the horizontal plane, are given by the lines A C, B D, which are, respectively, parallel to the two tangents at the flame brought through the centre of the lens. In the vertical plane, it may be said that these limits are marked by the lines Q R and S T, which are, respectively, parallel to the two lines passing through the centre of the

FIG. 13.

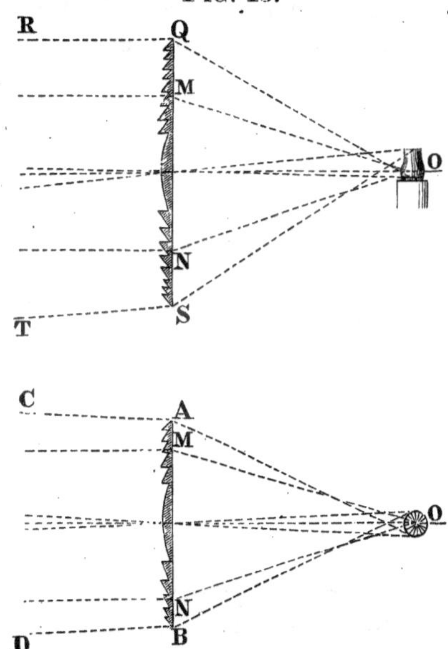

lens, and the one through the most elevated, and the other through the lowest point of the flame. All the rays which have their point of departure above the focus give dipping lights; those which have their point of departure below the focus are sent back towards the upper parts of the atmosphere.

When the drum is circular, in place of being polygonal, the lenses are cylindrical, and not annular. The luminous rays are distributed uniformly in the horizontal plane, and they act in a meridian section in the same way as those of the annular lenses.

The section of the luminous beam presents an inverted image of the flame on that side of the point where the ascending and descending rays cross each other. The angular amplitude of that image, referred to the focus, is in the inverse proportion to the actual dimensions; they diminish as the distance increases, and it, therefore, results that it is not indifferent, in the photometric operations, to take a short or a great distance from the lens whose effects are to be determined. The intensities will be found greater when further off, if the thickness of the atmosphere does not cause differences in the results. Thus, at the time when the experiments were made, with precision, in 1852, in the galleries of the wine-vaults at Paris, the intensities, as proved by the photometer, augmented to a distance varying from 80 to 150 metres, but they diminished in the reverse manner, which would have been produced if the atmosphere had been entirely transparent.

The figures below give some idea of the variation of amplitude and of brilliancy of the luminous beam emanating from an annular lens of the first order, embracing the eighth of the circumference, according as it is measured, at 25 metres or 100 metres from the focal point.

FIG. 14.

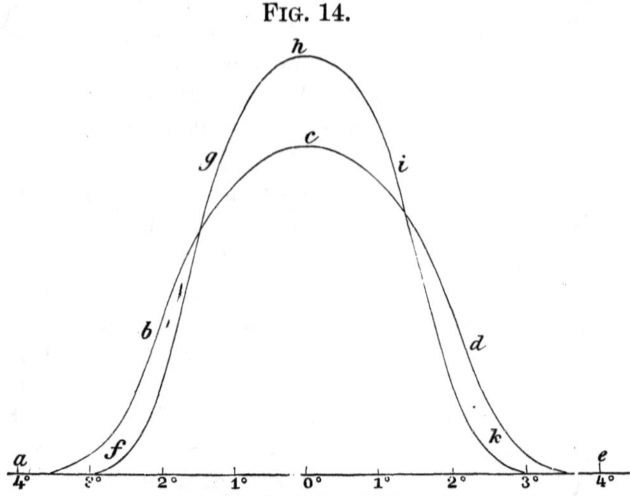

The curves *a b c d e*, *f g h i k*, of the Figure 14, represent the luminous rays in the horizontal plane most illuminated. The degrees are carried on the axis of the abscissæ, and the luminous intensities upon those of the ordinates, upon a scale of one centimeter for one thousand burners. The first of these curves is taken at 25 metres distance, and the second at 100 metres.

FIG. 15.

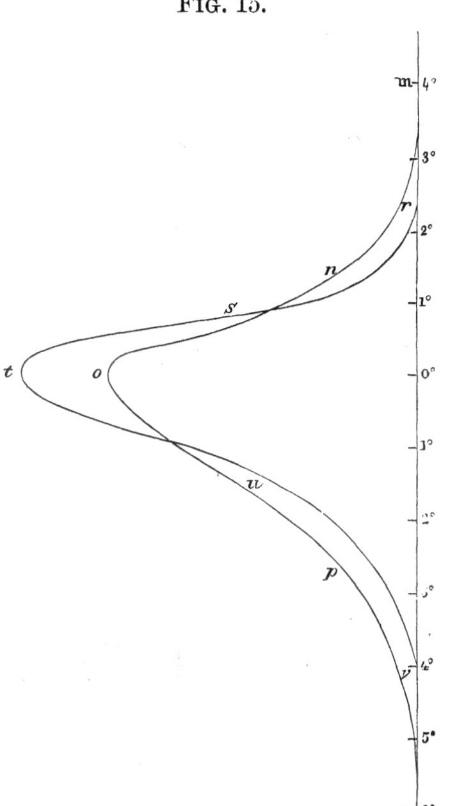

The curves *m n o p q*, *r s t u v*, of the Figure 15, upon the same scale, and also taken at 25 metres and 100 metres, show how the rays are distributed in the vertical plane passing through the focus and the axis of the lens.

All of these lines have been traced from the mean results deduced from numerous experiments, and often making allowance for slight anomalies.* Starting from the distance of 100 metres, the variations of amplitude, and, consequently, of intensity, are little marked, and it was not thought necessary to go beyond, for fear of losing too much influence by the default of transparency of the atmosphere. It is then at that limit at which have been taken the measures relative to the different apparatus which will be given further on.

* It seems necessary to show how these photometric experiments have been made. The method habitually employed consists in comparing the shadows thrown upon a table or white screen by an object which illuminates the two lights under test. The two lights are moved nearer or further away until they appear to be of the same shade, and the comparative luminous intensities are calculated according to the law of the square of the distances. That instrument has the great merit of being improvised at any time. A sheet of paper and a pencil is all that is required to construct it, but it has the inconvenience of failing in precision, for the reason that the observer finds difficulty in placing himself exactly between the two shadows, and in a normal direction to that of the table, and that, besides the determination of the line of the space, which is well illuminated, from which the dark shadows are detached, depends, in a certain degree, upon the delicacy or acuteness of the vision of the observer.

The photometer used in the service of the Commission of Lights was constructed by the engineer, Degrand, to the comparison of moveabie shadows; he substituted those of luminous bands, thrown upon a black surface. It is represented by the

The results are sensibly the same, with the exception as to the inclination of the rays, so far as the axis of the flame coincides with that of the apparatus, and that of the focus of the lens is situated in the interior of that flame. The preceding figure will then show how the flame ought to be placed with reference to the optical focus, according to the end proposed. If the condition was to oppose it to the dispersion of the luminous rays above the horizontal plane, the point below the flame will be the one which the focus should occupy; that will be the most brilliant which corresponds to the zero of the figure if it be desired to illuminate to the greatest possible distance on the horizontal plane. It will soon be seen how to place this point with reference to the focus, according to the height of the light-house above the level of the sea.

---

figures above, (16,) in section and elevation, and may be described as follows: The rays emanating from each light L l are received upon a pane, $m\ n\ m'\ n'$, covered by a sheet of paper or a coat of lacca, after having passed through an opening $p\ p'$, operated in the axis of a vertical screen, interposed between the pane of glass and

Fig. 16.

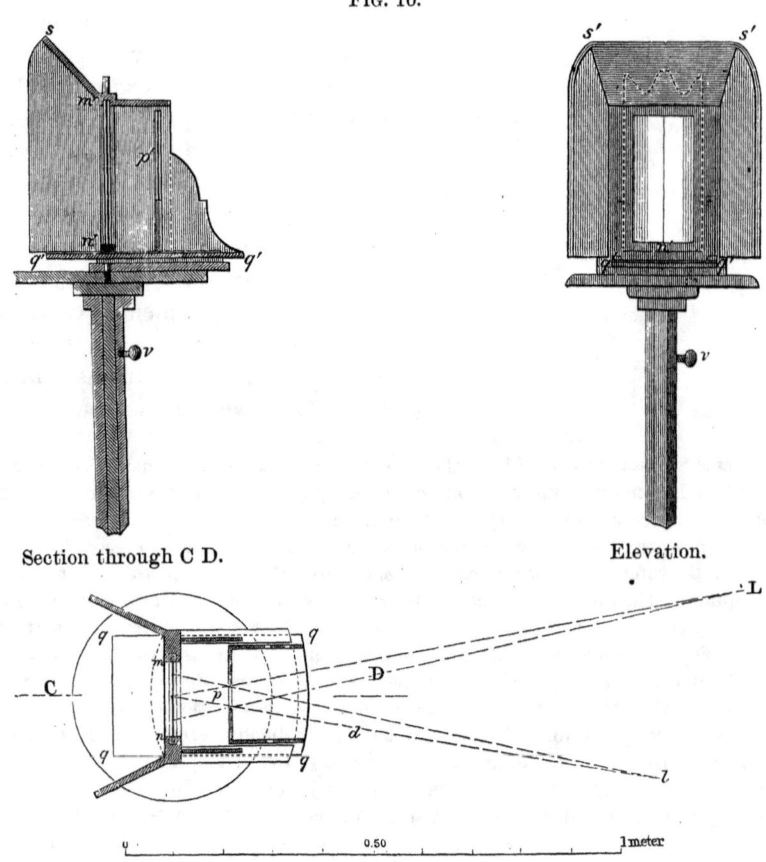

Section through C D.

Elevation.

After having been reflected by the catadioptric rings, the rays emanating from those parts of the flame situated above or below the optical focus act in the inverse way to those which return from the dioptric lenses. The first, as M N P, M N′ P′, (Fig. 17,) are directed towards the heavens; the second, such as Q N R, Q N′ R′, are brought down below the horizontal plane. In this way calculation is made of the greatest part of these rings for other optical focii besides those of the dioptric lens.

FIG. 17.

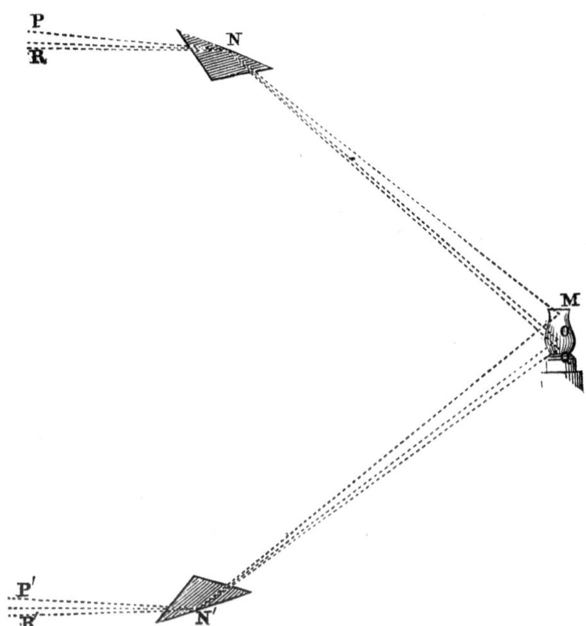

In each direction in which the flame of a lamp is seen, corresponds a thin section of maximum intensity, where it may be supposed the light is uniformly distributed, and whose centre of gravity ought to be

---

the lights. The observer places himself on the other side of the pane of glass, which is moved further from, or nearer, to compare the intensities of the two luminous bands or beams which are seen. The band or beam seen to the right is produced by the light L, and the other by the light l. The screen may be moved, which is placed upon a board, $q\ q\ q'\ q'$, which moves between two grooves, according as it may be found to be most convenient, to place the bands in contact, or to open them more, as they become more dim or brighter, from the illumination of the two focii. It is essential that the rays emanating from both lights should be equally inclined upon the pane of glass, and that will be assured of, and that condition fulfilled, when the line of separation of the two bands blends with a vertical dividing the pane into two equal parts. For that purpose the photometer is turned upon the plane which supports it. It is equally necessary that the two lights and the centre of the pane be on the same horizontal plane, and the instrument may be raised or lowered, at will, by means of a support, which slides in a case or sheath, and is maintained there by a screw, v. Every part of the photometer is painted in dead black, so as to prevent reflections of the luminous rays, and a large black curtain fixed at its upper part, $s\ s'\ s'$, permits the observer to completely isolate himself. The distances to be measured are those of the lights to the centre of the pane of glass. In designating them by D and d, we have—

$$L = l\ \frac{D^2}{d^2}.$$

taken for the focus of the ring situated on that side. Doubtless, neither the position nor the limits of that brilliant part is susceptible of being recognized with much precision, for it depends upon the form and constitution of the flame, which are variable and irregular; but there is not such a difference of intensity between two rays starting from points very near the illuminating body as to make it of real interest to obtain a rigorous solution of the problem.

The focii of the rings under discussion have been determined in the following manner: the flame has been placed in the middle of the dioptric drum of the apparatus in such a way that the centre of the horizontal section of the greatest brilliancy coincides nearly with the optical focus; after that, the focii to be assigned to the rings are fixed in accordance with considerations which are to be discussed. In this way it was determined to adopt the same focus for all the catadioptric upper rings, and to establish them in the lights of the two first orders at 0.01 above those of the dioptric lenses.

The foci of the rings placed below the lenticular drum have been raised now, because no account could be taken of the luminous rays which the lamp burner intercepted. Their height above the dioptric focus of one ring to another has been varied from 0.010*m.* to 0.035*m.* for the first order, to 0.032*m.* for the second, to 0.022*m.* for the third, and between the limits much more restricted for the apparatus of less dimensions. The same considerations have allowed other profiles, of which an account will be given further on, for the apparatus illuminated by oil of schiste, petroleum, or an electric current.

The profiles of Plate 3 exhibit very neatly the tracings of our principal apparatus. The Figures 1, 2, and 3 apply, respectively, to the first, second, and third orders, and the Figures 4, 5, and 6 to the apparatus of 0.50*m.*, of 0.375*m.*, and of 0.30*m.* in diameter, illuminated by colza oil. Figure 7 is that of an apparatus for schiste oil. Figures 8, 9, 10, and 11 give the profiles of the lenses of vertical elements corresponding to the dioptric drums of the four largest.

Experience has proved that the different sections of the apparatus thus disposed, transmit, horizontally, or rather following a little inclination, the most brilliant part of the beam generated, when the flame which illuminates them occupies the position, and has received the development which has served as the basis for the determination of the optical focii. It is easy to see that, if it has not fulfilled that condition, there will be a loss of luminous rays which will be still greater when it is separated more from the normal state.

DIRECTIONS TO GIVE TO THE LUMINOUS BEAMS.

It is not in the horizontal plane that the most brilliant part of the luminous beam should be directed, it is tangentially to the horizon of the sea; that is to say, following the generations of a conic surface having its summit at the focus of the apparatus, and generated by the rotation around the vertical axis passing through that point of the curve which determines the atmospheric refraction. (Fig. 2, page 28.)

The following table shows the inclination of the tangents for different heights above the level of the sea, and it indicates, besides, how high the focus ought to be raised above the axis of the dioptric lens, so that the most intense part of the beam emanating from that lens follows the desired direction:

Height of the luminous focus above the surface of the sea, H (in metres.)	Distance from the point of contact of the luminous ray tangent to the surface of the sea, $D=\sqrt{\frac{R.\ H.}{0.42}}$, R=6,366,953 (in metres.)	Inclination of the luminous rays touching the horizon, $\tan a=\frac{0.84\,D}{R}$.	Raising of the focal centre, (in millimetres,) for apparatus in which F =				
			0.92*m*.	0.70*m*.	0.50*m*.	0.25*m*.	0.15*m*.
		′ ″					
5	8,706	3.57	1.1	0.8	0.6	0.3	0.2
10	12,312	5.35	1.5	1.1	0.8	0.4	0.2
15	15,079	6.50	1.8	1.4	1.0	0.5	0.3
20	17,412	7.54	2.1	1.6	1.1	0.6	0.3
25	19,468	8.50	2.4	1.8	1.3	0.6	0.4
30	21,326	9.40	2.6	2.0	1.4	0.7	0.4
35	23,034	10.27	2.8	2.1	1.5	0.8	0.5
40	24,625	11.10	3.0	2.3	1.6	0.8	0.5
45	26,118	11.51	3.2	2.4	1.7	0.9	0.5
50	27,531	12.29	3.3	2.5	1.8	0.9	0.5
55	28,875	13.6	3.5	2.7	1.9	1.0	0.6
60	30,159	13.41	3.7	2.8	2.0	1.0	0.6
65	31,390	14.14	3.8	2.9	2.1	1.0	0.6
70	32,575	14.46	4.0	3.0	2.1	1.1	0.6
75	33,719	15.18	4.1	3.1	2.2	1.1	0.7
80	34,825	15.48	4.2	3.2	2.3	1.1	0.7
85	35,896	16.17	4.4	3.3	2.4	1.2	0.7
90	36,937	16.45	4.5	3.4	2.4	1.2	0.7
95	37,949	17.13	4.6	3.5	2.5	1.3	0.8
100	38,935	17.40	4.7	3.6	2.6	1.3	0.8
105	39,897	18.6	4.8	3.7	2.6	1.3	0.8
110	40,835	18.31	5.0	3.8	2.7	1.3	0.8
115	41,753	18.56	5.1	3.9	2.8	1.4	0.8
120	42,651	19.20	5.2	3.9	2.8	1.4	0.8
125	43,531	19.45	5.3	4.0	2.9	1.4	0.9
130	44,393	20.8	5.4	4.1	2.9	1.5	0.9
135	45,238	20.31	5.5	4.2	3.0	1.5	0.9
140	46,069	20.54	5.6	4.3	3.0	1.5	0.9
145	46,884	21.16	5.7	4.3	3.1	1.5	0.9
150	47,686	21.38	5.8	4.4	3.1	1.6	0.9
155	48,474	21.59	5.9	4.5	3.2	1.6	1.0
160	49,249	22.20	6.0	4.5	3.2	1.6	1.0
165	50,013	22.41	6.1	4.6	3.3	1.6	1.0
170	50,765	23.1	6.2	4.7	3.3	1.7	1.0
175	51,506	23.22	6.3	4.8	3.4	1.7	1.0
180	52,237	23.41	6.3	4.8	3.4	1.7	1.0
185	52,957	24.1	6.4	4.9	3.5	1.7	1.0
190	53,668	24.20	6.5	5.0	3.5	1.8	1.1
195	54,370	24.40	6.6	5.0	3.6	1.8	1.1
200	55,063	24.58	6.7	5.1	3.6	1.8	1.1
205	55,747	25.17	6.8	5.1	3.7	1.8	1.1
210	56,422	25.35	6.8	5.2	3.7	1.9	1.1

Inclination of the tangents, &c.—Continued.

Height of the luminous focus above the surface of the sea, H (in metres.)	Distance from the point of contact of the luminous ray tangent to the surface of the sea, $D=\sqrt{\frac{R.\ H.}{0.\ 42}}$, R=6,366,953 (in metres.)	Inclination of the luminous rays touching the horizon, $\text{tang } a=\frac{0.84D}{R}$.	Raising of the focal centre, (in millimetres,) for apparatus in which F=				
			0.92*m*.	0.70*m*.	0.50*m*.	0.25*n*.	0.15*m*.
		′ ″					
215	57,090	25.54	6.9	5.3	3.8	1.9	1.1
220	57,750	26.12	7.0	5.3	3.8	1.9	1.1
225	58,403	26.29	7.1	5.4	3.9	1.9	1.2
230	59,048	26.47	7.2	5.5	3.9	1.9	1.2
235	59,686	27.4	7.2	5.5	3.9	2.0	1.2
240	60,318	27.21	7.3	5.6	4.0	2.0	1.2
245	60,943	27.38	7.4	5.6	4.0	2.0	1.2
250	61,562	27.55	7.5	5.7	4.1	2.0	1.2
255	62,174	28.12	7.5	5.7	4.1	2.1	1.2
260	62,781	28.28	7.6	5.8	4.1	2.1	1.2
265	63,382	28.45	7.7	5.9	4.2	2.1	1.3
270	63,977	29.1	7.8	5.9	4.2	2.1	1.3
275	64,567	29.17	7.8	6.0	4.3	2.1	1.3
280	65,151	29.33	7.9	6.0	4.3	2.1	1.3
285	65,730	29.49	8.0	6.1	4.3	2.2	1.3
290	66,304	30.4	8.0	6.1	4.4	2.2	1.3
295	66,873	30.20	8.1	6.2	4.4	2.2	1.3
300	67,438	30.35	8.2	6.2	4.4	2.2	1.3

If it be designed to operate with rigorous correctness, it will be necessary to have varied with the height of the apparatus above the level of the sea: 1st, the position of the lamp with reference to the base of the lenticular drum; 2d, the inclination of the dioptric lenses; 3d, the profile of the catadioptric rings. But, with regard to the habitual elevation of the lights, and to the dimensions as well as to the oscillations of the flame, the two first modifications are not really necessary except in exceptional circumstances and cases, and it is scarcely ever thought necessary to have recourse to this last.

POSITION OF THE FLAME IN APPARATUS OF THE FIRST ORDER.

Whenever the flame of an apparatus of the first order has received the development and the brilliancy of which it is susceptible—that is to say, when it has 0.10*m*. of height, and has become white in the greater part of its circumference—the most brilliant zone commences at 0.015*m*. about above the crown of the burner, and extends itself to about 0.050*m*. above the same point. The position of the lamp in the interior of the apparatus is regulated accordingly. In all the lights of that order, whose height above the level of the sea is comprised between 45 metres and 100 metres, and these are the most numerous, the burner is placed at 0.028*m.* below the focus of the dioptric lenses, which places it at 0.038*m.* of the upper catadioptric rings. The luminous beam of the greatest intensity coming from the apparatus complete, whatever otherwise the character of the light, is slightly inclined towards the horizon, following the angle which varies with the degree of perfection of the mounting of the prisms, and the oscillations of the flame, and more of the rays are carried below than above the horizontal plane.

FIG. 18.

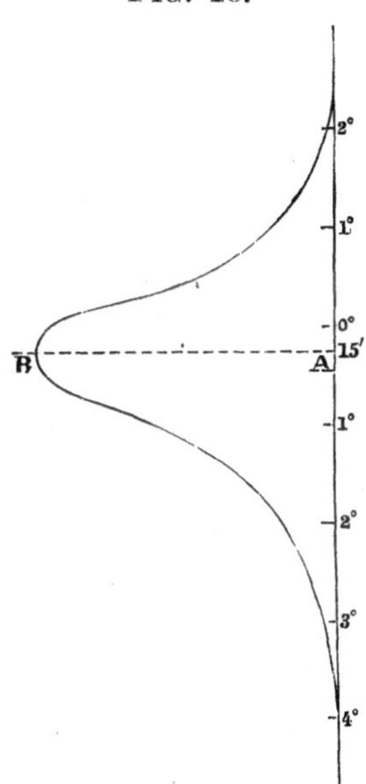

It is evident that that angle cannot be determined with great precision; neither the process of construction, nor the practical means of verifying the apparatus permit it; but it is, however, authorized to be admitted within, that it is about 15 minutes, when the apparatus is treated with the degree of precision which our able constructors know so well how to obtain. But in the lights under consideration, the lines thus inclined may be considered as tangents to the surface of the sea; the error of which they are liable may be entirely neglected.

An example will illustrate this point, which is essential and has not always been understood. The Figure 18 shows how the illuminous rays emanate from a complete apparatus of the first-order fixed light, distributing themselves in the vertical plane above and below the dioptric focus, when the burner of the lamp is fixed at 0.028*m.* below that point, and of a flame fully developed. The angular spaces have been carried upon the axis of the ordinates on a scale of 0.01*m.* per degree, and the intensities are expressed upon the axis of the abscissæ on the scale of 0.01*m.* for 200 burners. The focus of the apparatus is placed at zero of the axis. The most intense part of the beam A B makes with the horizon an angle of about 15 minutes. The rays above are projected towards the heaven; all those which are below, and those are the most numerous, cut the surface of the sea, when the height of the light is a mean between the limits spoken of.

FORM OF A LUMINOUS BEAM.

The following figure is of a kind to give an idea of the subject. It represents the real form of the section through a vertical plane passing through the focus of the luminous beam from an apparatus of a first-order fixed light, in that which we may consider as a mean state of the atmosphere, that is to say, when the light of unity reaches to 7 kilometres. The distances are recorded on a scale of 0.007*m.* per nautical mile. At F is the focus, and the line of the greatest luminous intensity, F O, is that which ought to be directed tangentially to the horizon. The part of the luminous beam situated above that line is lost to the mariner, and that which is placed below a line reaches the surface of the sea.

FIG. 19.

It is seen, then, in what proportion the range will be reduced if it is wished to utilize the whole of the light sent by the apparatus, and it is also seen that the curve is sufficiently flattened at its summit for a variation of some minutes in the direction of the line F O, not to exert a sensible influence upon the range of the light.

MODIFICATIONS TO INTRODUCE IN THE APPARATUS BECAUSE OF THE HEIGHT OF THE FOCAL PLANE.

Modifications become necessary when the focal plane of the light-house is more than 100 metres above the level of the sea, and they are of two kinds—those relative to the luminous beam passing through the lenticular drum, and the others to those reflected by the catadioptric rings.

In those which relate to the drum, the burner of the lamp is raised, according to the height of the focal plane and conformably to the figures inserted in the foregoing table, in such a manner as to have the beams properly inclined. But the distance 0.028*m.* of the crown of the burner at the centre of the drum, being established in view of a mean elevation of about 70 metres, ought not to be reduced more than the difference existing between the figures of the table and those which correspond to that latter height, 0.004*m.* Thus, for a light having 150 metres above the level of the sea, the crown of the burner should be held at 0.028*m.*—(0.0058*m.*—0.0040*m.*) = 0.0262*m.* below the horizontal plane passing through the centre of the drum. A loss of light results from the form of the lenses, but it is insignificant in the practical limits.

In the eclipse lights whose elevations are very considerable, such as that of Cape Carbon in Algeria, which is 220 metres, the lenses of the drum are inclined in such a manner as to render them normal to the line directed tangentially to the horizon, and the burner of that light is placed at 0.028*m.* + 0.004*m.*, which is 0.032*m.* below the focus. The drum presents the form of a truncated pyramid. This can only be done in fixed apparatus, because it will be necessary to give a conical form to the drum, from which would result difficulties of construction which would not be sufficiently justified. Moreover, great heights above the level of the sea are rarely selected, for the reason that very high points are subject to being covered or obscured by fogs.

In raising the burner, the catadioptric parts of the apparatus are operated upon inversely to that upon which it acts upon the drum; it causes the luminous beam to be above in place of lowering it upon the horizon, and it becomes necessary to calculate a special profile for each height if it is desired to proceed with the greatest accuracy. This would be a serious inconvenience, but the problem may be solved more simply, and with the degree of rigorous accuracy which the subject requires. Is the question one of a ring for a fixed light? Each of its parts is gently inclined in such a way that the mean inclination of the reflecting face of each fragment is directed upon the horizon and above the most intense beam. Is it a catadioptric annular panel such as those used for eclipse lights? A movement is given to it analogous to that required for the dioptric panel of the drum. It is easy to understand that approximate solutions are admissible without difficulty in similar cases, and that an extreme precision will at the same time be without any real object, on account of the incessant modifications which are taking place in the state of the flame.

Fig. 20.

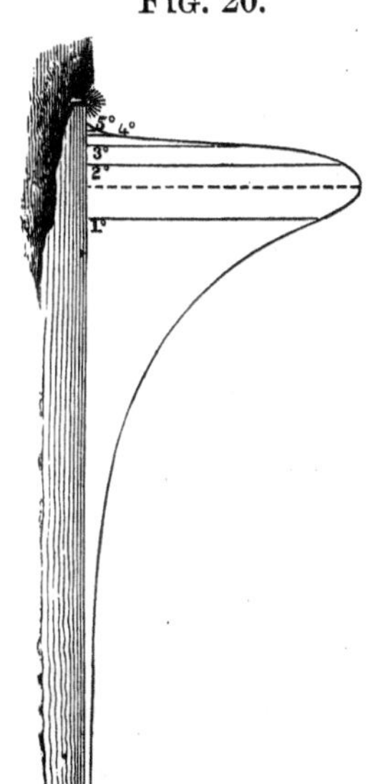

VARIATION OF THE LUMINOUS INTENSITY WITH THE DISTANCE.

It is to be remarked that, although the beam having the greatest intensity is directed to the limit of the horizon, the quantity of light seen by the navigator increases in augmentation in starting from this point, in proportion as the light is approached, then to diminish, and soon after disappear. Figure 20 shows the distribution of the luminous intensities of a fixed light of the first order, whose focal plane is 60 metres above the level of the sea. The distances are laid down on a scale of 0.007*m.* per nautical mile upon the axis of the abscissæ, and the quantities of light are carried upon the axis of the ordinates on a scale of 0.10*m.* per hundred (100) burners. It is seen that, in the state of the atmosphere taken as the basis of the calculations, it is to about 1.08 miles from the foot of the light-house that the light appears most brilliant to the eyes of the navigators. The tangent point of the luminous beam is at O.

POSITION OF THE FLAME IN THE APPARATUS OF THE SECOND, THIRD, AND FOURTH ORDER.

The same means are taken into consideration in directing tangentially to the surface of the sea the most intense part of the luminous beams emanating from the apparatus of the three other orders. With regard to the constitution of the flames of these apparatus, it is regulated so that it follows distance to be observed between the focus of the drum and the crown of the burner for mean heights:

Light of the 2d order: Mean height, 45*m.*; distance, 0.026*m.*

Light of the 3d order: Mean height, 25*m.*; distance, 0.024*m.*

Light of the 4th order: Mean height, 12*m.*; distance, 0.022*m.*

In those of the last lights, which are illuminated with the oil of schiste, the burner occupies another position, which will be shown when combustibles are treated of.

GENERAL DISPOSITIONS OF THE APPARATUS.

The apparatus for fixed lights of the first order is composed of eight panels in each of the three parts in which it is divided, and these panels are placed upon the same axes, as shown by Figure 2, Plate 6.

The largest annular lenses of the apparatus of the same order only embrace one-eighth of the circumference. They belong to the lights whose eclipses succeed each other every minute. The duration of the flash which they produce is very restricted, because of their little divergence, of eight seconds at a short distance; they diminish in proportion as the observer recedes from them. It is greater in the reflector lights, and that merit is highly appreciated by mariners. It would doubtless have been easy to remedy the inconvenience which the new system presented, for it would only have been required to render the lenses more divergent; but more would have been lost in intensity than would have been gained in duration, and that would have been a bad solution of the question.

The same result has been obtained by not placing the annular catadioptric panels upon the same axes as the dioptric panels; they are deviated a little, as shown in Figure 4 of Plate 5, and Figure 2 of Plate 7, in such a way that the flashes follow each other in place of being superposed. They first make an angle of 4° with the seconds in horizontal projection, and they precede them in the sense of the rotation movement. The navigator sees at first the flash of the catadioptric panel, and then the flash of the brilliant dioptric panel. The figure below shows the variations of the intensities of the total flash; it is shown on a scale of 0.01*m.* to the degree, and 0.001*m.* to 100 burners.

The curve A B C D E is that of the distribution of the luminous rays emanating from the dioptric panel in the plane of the greatest intensity, and the curve F G H I J that of the catadioptric panel. The intensities join in the place where they are superposed, and the

FIG. 21.

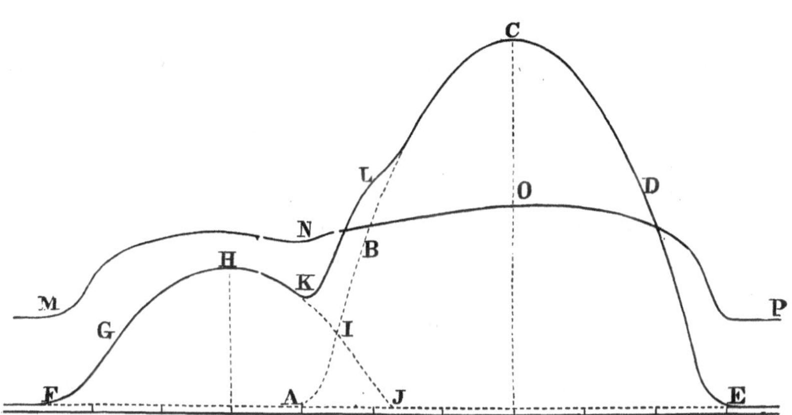

curve F G H K L C D E represents the effect produced by the two united panels. There is a point of inflexion, and the height of the first curve extends notably beyond the second. It might be feared, on one side, that the flash would be separated by an eclipse of a kind to deceive the navigators as to the character of the light; and on the other, that the benefit of prolongation would not be assured but upon a small part of the illuminated extent. But the curve of the ranges answers to the intensities in the different directions in which it is represented by the line M N O P, which is represented on a scale of 0.001*m.* per nautical mile, exhibited in such a way that the errors are sufficiently small to be left out of the account.

The lower catadioptric rings are not arranged in panels in the lights now under consideration; they are for fixed lights, as were produced by the parabolic mirrors of the old apparatus.

The same dispositions may be adopted for the nearer eclipse lights. It will be sufficient to cause the revolving motion to increase in the inverse ratio of the duration of the intervals to be observed between the luminous apparitions; but the duration of the flashes will be reduced in the same proportion, and it is preferred to multiply the lenses, although the intensities are thus diminished in nearly the same degree.

The apparatus of the first order, whose eclipses reproduce themselves in every thirty seconds, have sixteen panels in its circumference instead of eight. When the flashes succeed each other at shorter intervals, of twenty to twenty seconds, and below that, the attempt to prolong the duration is given up for fear of reducing too greatly the power, and at the same time suffers the fixed light to add to them, reunited in beams, the luminous rays which would have constituted it, three annular panels are superposed upon the same axis.

Three principal systems are employed to produce what is called the fixed light varied by flashes, of which are the fixed lights which present white or colored flashes at regular intervals of time, more or less intense. These flashes are sometimes preceded and followed by eclipses of short duration.

The first of these systems consists in causing several lenses of vertical elements to revolve in front from a fixed-light apparatus. These lenses are of the same height as the dioptric drum, and produce concurrently with it an effect analogous to that of an annular lens; they bring together in a beam the luminous rays which, without their interposition would be distributed uniformly in the angular space which they subtend. An eclipse precedes the flash, and another follows it. They are not total except at great distances from the light-house, because the movable lenses only cover the drum without extinguishing the rays brought from catadioptric rings.

The Figures 5, 8, 12, and 15 of Plate 1, give an idea of the distribution of the luminous rays in apparatus of this sort.

There are no lenses of vertical elements in the second system. The drum of the apparatus of the fixed light is cut by a certain number of annular lenses at equal distances, and the revolving motion is given to the entire drum, sometimes even to the whole apparatus, when in a light of the lower orders. The luminous appearances are the same as in the preceding combination. Preference is given to one or the other disposition, according as the apparatus is to illuminate the whole or only a part of the horizon. In the last case, the lens of vertical elements serves best, because it allows a reduction of the angular space in the fixed apparatus in which the luminous rays should be sent out, leaving an open space to facilitate the service of the keeper, and does not require so heavy a weight to put it in motion. But there is an advantage, in the first hypothesis, to employ the annular lenses, for the reason that there is economy in the expense of the establishment, and at the same time economy of light, since the rays which produce the flashes have but one lens traverse instead of two.

The apparatus of the third system have no eclipses. They are composed of two parts upon their heights, which are established, one after the manner of the fixed light apparatus, the other like those for eclipses.

This last only is put in motion, when the apparatus is not required to illuminate the entire horizon, and is placed above the other.

The Figures 7, 8, and 9 of Plate 5 represent one of the apparatus of the third order.

When it is desired to color the flashes, each of the panels which produce them is covered by a colored pane of glass, and also add to them habitually small thin sheets of the same glass, which change the color of the fixed white light during the entire duration of the flash.

The same figures, and those of Plate 10, furnish examples of that disposition of the apparatus.

APPARATUS OF THE LOWER ORDERS.

The apparatus of the smaller orders are disposed in the same manner as those of the first order, according to the effects which are desired to be obtained, but they do not in general carry an equally large number of panels.

APPARATUS FOR THE ELECTRIC LIGHT.

The relation which it is necessary to observe between the dimensions of the apparatus and that of the illuminating body which occupies the focus, under pain of erring by excess or by default of divergence, at least to have recourse to the special profiles, allow the use of apparatus of more restricted dimensions, that is to say, those of 0.30*m*., for lights to be illuminated by the electric light. A flame of that kind has no more than from 0.01*m*. or 0.012*m*. to 0.015*m*. of elevation, and the divergence in the vertical plane of one of these small apparatus is only about 6°; it is very near that of an apparatus of the first order, as has been found by experiment.

It has been determined, besides, that it was necessary to have recourse to new dispositions for the catadioptric rings of the apparatus. They have been calculated for the same focus as the lens, and the manner to return the luminous rays, not horizontally, but tangentially, to the surface of the sea.

Finally, the smallness of the electric flame does not allow of the prolonging of the uprights of the armature in the entire height of the apparatus, for they would almost totally obscure it, and at the same time would direct the joints and indented work of the lenticular profile of the apparatus, not in following the horizontals, as is done ordinarily, but according to the direction which is taken in the interior of the glass after a first refraction of the rays emanating from the focus.

The Figure 22 represents an apparatus of a fixed light disposed in view of the new mode of producing light.

APPARATUS FOR OIL OF SCHISTE, OR PETROLEUM.

The form of the flames produced by the oil of schiste, or of petroleum, also requires special apparatus. The Profile 7 of Plate 3 has been established for double current of air lamps, as those whose burner and flame are represented by Figure 10 of Plate 15. The centre of the flame, or rather that of the mushroom, has been taken for the focus of dioptric lenses, and the focus of the catadioptric rings has been placed at the same height, but to 0.017*m*. of the axis, upon the side of the flame the most distant from the profile for the high, and upon the side the nearest for the first of those below. The focus of the lower ring has been more eccentric still, and carried to 0.019*m*. of the axis. It is seen that these dispositions have for effect to bring back the greater part of the luminous rays in the horizontal plane and below. The little height of the flame renders also the divergence in the vertical plane notably inferior to that which is produced by apparatus of the same order, illuminated by colza oil; and for the joints of the dioptric profile, a disposition has been adopted analogous to that which was referred to in speaking of the electric light.

FIG. 22.

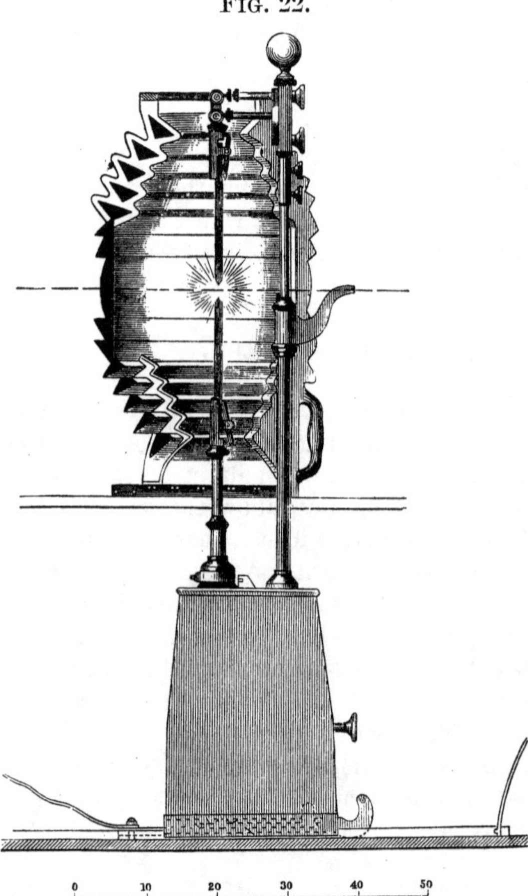

It is understood that the lens apparatus is susceptible of extremely varied forms, and it belongs to the engineers to adopt, in each particular case, those which appear the best adapted to the circumstances. Further on, numerous examples will be given.

LUMINOUS INTENSITIES OF THE DIFFERENT PARTS OF THE APPARATUS.

The intensities of the luminous beams emitted from the principal parts of the different orders of apparatus may be estimated, in practice, as indicated in the following table. The first gives the intensities in the axis, and the second the intensities on each side of the axis, for the dioptric annular lenses, the most generally used:

Intensities of the luminous beams in the axis of the apparatus.

Indication of the apparatus.	Intensity.			
	Of the lamp only	Of the upper catadioptric cupola.	Of the central lens.	Of the lower catadioptric crown.
Cylindrical lenses of fixed lights.	*Burners.*	*Burners.*	*Burners.*	*Burners.*
1st order	23	130	440	60
2d order	15	70	240	25
3d order, large model	5	18	65	7
3d order, small model	3	6	21.5	2.5
4th order, (0.375*m.*)	1.6	2.7	9.3	1
4th order, (0.375*m.*,) for schiste oil	2.2	4.5	17.5	2
4th order, (0.30*m.*)	1.3	1.8	6.4	0.8
4th order, (0.30*m.*,) for schiste oil	2.2	3.5	13	1.5
4th order, (0.30*m.*,) electric light	125	750	2000	750
Annular lenses of revolving lights.				
1st order, 1-8	23	1900	5016	875
1st order, 1-16	23	950	2465	430
1st order, 1-24	23	600	1600	275
2d order, 1-8	15	925	2525	360
2d order, 1-12	15	600	1650	235
2d order, 1-20	15	355	960	135
3d order, large pattern, 1-8	5	315	838	113
3d order, large pattern, 1-10	5	250	665	90
3d order, large pattern, 1-12	5	200	543	74
3d order, large pattern, 1-16	5	140	400	50
3d order, small pattern, 1-6	3	80	235	30
3d order, small pattern, 1-10	3	45	130	18
Lenses with vertical elements for lights varied by flashes.				
1st order, 7 elements, 34° 12′	23	1110	3810	530
2d order, 9 elements, 43° 40′	15	740	2605	300
3d order, 7 elements, 44° 32′	5	265	925	100
3d order, small pattern, 5 elements, 50°	3	60	230	25
4th order. (0.375*m.*,) 5 elements, 61° 34′	1.6	34	115	12
4th order, (0.375*m.*,) for schiste, 5 elements, 61° 34′	2.2	60	215	20

Intensities of the luminous beams on each side of the axis of the apparatus.

Angle measured to parts of the axis.	Annular dioptric lenses.									
	1st order.			2d order.			3d order.			
							Large model.		Small model.	
	1-8	1-16	1-24	1-8	1-12	1-20	1-8	1-12	1-6	1-10
° ′	*Burners.*	*Burners.*	*Burners.*	*Burners.*	*Burn rs.*	*Burn's.*	*Burn's.*	*Burn's.*	*Burn's.*	*Burn's.*
0	5015	2465	1600	2525	1650	960	838	543	235	130
0. 30	4855	2340	1550	2445	1600	930	805	520	232	128
1	4375	2150	1395	2205	1440	840	704	456	223	123
1. 30	3575	1750	1140	1800	1175	695	538	347	206	114
2	2450	1210	785	1235	810	470	302	195	184	102
2. 30	1010	500	325	525	335	195	....	....	154	85
2. 45	....	....	....	....	....	....	0	0	....	....
3	0	0	0	0	0	0	....	....	120	67
4	....	....	....	....	....	....	....	....	31	18
4. 30	....	....	....	....	....	....	....	....	0	0

The figures of these two tables have been established by reducing of about one-tenth those which have been obtained in our experiments, to compensate for the practical imperfections, besides in diminishing the results one-tenth more, on account of the absorption of the plate glass of the lantern.

MODE OF CONSTRUCTING THE LENSES.

The glass of Saint Gobain is used exclusively in the construction of our lenses. The manufacture has been greatly improved within a few years, and leaves but little to be desired now. It is free from color, hard, homogeneous, and absorbs but a small portion of the rays which pass through it; takes a very beautiful polish; resists the action of the atmosphere perfectly, and contains but a very small number of air bubbles, or of striæ. Its composition is actually as follows:

Silica....................................	72.1
Soda....................................	12.2
Chalk....................................	15.7
Alumina and oxid of iron, traces....................	
	100.0

Its index of refraction, which was formerly 1.50, has been actually raised to 1.54.

The glass is run into iron moulds of the proper dimensions for the required pieces to be worked, after which the unpolished glass is placed upon the turning lathes, put in motion by a steam engine, where it is turned in a way to give it the exact forms prescribed, and until a perfect polish is made. That operation takes time, and requires the services of skilled workmen.

The different parts which enter into the composition of the same lens are executed separately, afterwards cemented on their edges by means of a mastic, and are placed in bronze frames. The correctness of the work is determined by the method of conjugate focii. In calculating the lenses, regard is had to the reduction, as far as possible, of the thickness of the glass, so as to diminish the absorption of the luminous rays; but, in doing so, a certain limit cannot be exceeded for fear of failing to obtain the required solidity, of rendering the construction too difficult, and above all, of incurring too great expense.

These considerations, and the progress which has been made within a short time in the moulding of glass, have led Engineer Degrand to think that this last mode of construction may be advantageously applied to the establishment of lenses in echelon, which will allow the thickness to be considerably reduced. It is expanding the idea of Buffon, but with better incentives, and much greater chances of success.

The glass is run into the cast-iron moulds, turned with the greatest precision in regard to reëntering angles, and the small apparatus thus made have been very successful in their results. It has not, unfortunately, been so in others. The economy of luminous rays resulting from the reduction of the thickness of the glass has not compensated for the dispersion due to the irregularity of the surface, and, from all calculations made, it does not appear that the new process is susceptible of extension in the present state of glass manufacture.

The apparatus represented on the Plate 10, and by the Figures 5, 6, 7, and 8 of Plate 12, have been constructed of mould glass.

III.—COMPARISON OF THE TWO SYSTEMS OF APPARATUS.

The superiority of the dioptric apparatus to the catoptric will be seen by the following facts:

1st. The reflection upon the most highly polished metallic surfaces absorbs more of the luminous rays than the passage of those rays through lenses of a proper thickness.

2d. According to the dimensions in general use, which have been very judiciously adopted, the divergence of the luminous rays is very much greater in the catoptric apparatus than in the others, and a great part of that divergence cannot be utilized.

3d. The dioptric apparatus allows the distribution of the light uniformly upon the entire or only a part of the horizon, which cannot be properly done with the catoptric apparatus, unless by multiplying the reflectors out of proportion, except with those which have received the name of "Sideral Apparatus," which are not capable of producing a great luminous intensity.

4th. Flashes of much greater intensity are obtained from dioptric apparatus than from the most powerful catoptric apparatus.

These last apparatus possess always the advantage over the dioptric in the economy of expense in first fitting or establishing the lights; but this merit is nearly always counterbalanced by the great increase in annual expense of the catoptric, as compared with the dioptric lights. In other words, the useful effect of the dioptric apparatus is far beyond that of the catoptric, as will be shown by some examples.

Let us take, for comparison, not the quantity of light emanating from the apparatus, but that which is sent or brought into the horizontal plane. This last alone imports, in effect, as regards the object which we have in view, inasmuch as, directed, as it is said, tangentially to the surface of the sea, it determines the range of the light under ordinary circumstances of the atmosphere. It is evident, that no account can be taken of the rays thrown above the horizontal plane, for they are entirely lost. As for those which descend below, they are no doubt useful to the maritime illumination; but it is to be remarked that in all of our apparatus, being more numerous than would be rigorously necessary, since the apparent intensity of the light increases in proportion as the foot of the tower is approached, in the whole extent of the zone which it is required to illuminate. There is, it is true, some interest to have during foggy weather a great number of plunging rays, but it is known that under these atmospheric circumstances it is necessary to have an enormous difference between the intensities, to obtain a slight increase of range. Thus, the divergence below the horizontal plane becomes habitually useless so soon as it passes a certain limit, which is greatly affected in dioptric apparatus, and for which there is no real interest to look for in foggy weather. There is then authority to leave it out.

The useful effect of an illuminating apparatus may be deduced from the formula

$$\frac{L}{I+D},$$

in which L is designed to represent the quantity of light; by I the annual interest of the cost of the purchase; and by D the annual expense of keeping up the light, including the consumption of oil, wicks, chimneys, salaries of the keepers, keeping the apparatus in order, the repairs, &c. The cost of the unity of light sent to the horizon, is

$$\frac{I+D}{L}.$$

If the comparison between the apparatus of the two systems should be made the occasion of the establishment of a new light-house, it would be necessary to operate with exactness, include in the value of I the interest of the sum required, or that will be required, for the construction of the edifice.

APPARATUS OF THE FOURTH ORDER.

Let us first compare the small apparatus, illuminated by the same lamps, a reflector, (photophore,) a "sideral" apparatus, and an apparatus of mould glass, such as is represented by Figure 6, Plate 12, each enclosed in a small movable lantern, and allow that the two last ought to illuminate the entire circumference. The quantity of light sent to the horizon by the "photophore" should be represented by the sum of the mean intensities of each illuminated degree, and those which correspond to the other apparatus, should have for expression the product of the intensity multiplied by 360.

According to the following figures, the quantities of luminous rays distributed in the horizontal plane are:

For the photophore			1005 *b.*
For the sideral	3. 50 *b.*	× 360 =	1260
For the lens apparatus	6. 00	× 360 =	2160

The cost of the apparatus is as follows:

Photophore	350 *fr.*
Sideral	500
Lens apparatus	500

From which, for I, the values, respectively, 17. 50 *fr.*, 25. 00 *fr.*, and 25. 00 *fr.*, in allowing an interest of five per cent.

The annual expense of maintenance may be estimated as follows:

For the photophore:

Expense of oil, 0.050 *kg.* × 4000 + 20 = 220 *kg.*, at 1.51 *fr.* =	332. 20 *fr.*
Salary and fuel for one keeper	570. 00
Wicks, chimneys, and different supplies	38. 00
Care of the apparatus, &c., repairs, &c	70. 00
Total	1010. 20

For the sideral:

Expense of oil, 0.045 *kg.* × 4000 + 20 = 200 *kg.*, at 1. 51 *fr.* =	302. 00 *fr.*
Salary and fuel for one keeper	570. 00
Wicks, chimneys, and different supplies	40. 00
Care of apparatus, &c., repairs, &c	80. 00
Total	992. 00

For the lens apparatus:

Expense of oil, 0.050 *kg.* × 4000 + 20 = 220 *kg.*, at 1.51 *fr.* =	332. 20 *fr.*
Salary and fuel for one keeper	570. 00
Wicks, chimneys, and different supplies	42. 00
Care of the apparatus, &c., repairs, &c	80. 00
Total	1024. 20

From which may be taken:

For the photophore: $\frac{L}{I + D} = \frac{1005}{17.50 + 1010.20} = 0.9779.$

For the sideral: $\frac{1260}{25.00 + 992.00} = 1.2389.$

For the lens apparatus: $\frac{2160}{25.00 + 1024.20} = 2.0587.$

If the cost of unity of light is represented by 1 in the lens apparatus, it will be raised to 2. 11 if a photophore is used, and to 1. 66 with the sideral apparatus.

APPARATUS OF THE THIRD ORDER.

The quantity of light sent to the horizon by a dioptric apparatus of the third order, illuminating 360°, illuminated by a lamp consuming 175 grammes of oil, may be represented by L = 90 *b.* × 360 = 32,400 *b.*

The estimated cost of the apparatus and its lantern, is 22,290 *fr.* As follows:

Lens apparatus	9100. 00 *fr.*
Armature	1200. 00
Lamps	1100. 00
Different supplies	540. 00
Lantern, including glazing, and lightning conductor	8350. 00
Transportation and placing in position	2000. 00

From which, in calculating the interest at five per cent., and rejecting the cost of the buildings, I = 1114. 50 *fr.*

The annual expense of maintenance may be estimated as follows:

Expense of oil 0.175 *kg.*, × 4000 + 90 = 790 *kg.*, at 1. 51 *fr.*	1192. 90 *fr.*
Salaries and fuel for two keepers	1575. 00
Wicks, chimneys, and different supplies	112. 00
Care of apparatus, &c., repairs, &c.	260. 00
Total	3139. 90

Useful effect: $\frac{L}{I + D} = \frac{32400}{1114.50 + 3139.90} = 7.62.$

Cost of the unity of light: $\frac{I + D}{L} = 0.131$ *fr.*

It would be necessary to go completely beyond the adopted dimensions, and perhaps also of those which could be practically admitted, if it were desired to obtain with a sideral apparatus a luminous intensity nearly equivalent to that of the lens apparatus; but for that purpose reflectors made of one piece may be employed, provided the number is sufficiently large. Twenty-four reflectors of 0. 29*m.* of opening, illuminated by lamps consuming 50 grammes of oil per hour, being uniformly placed around the circumference, would give a fixed light whose intensity would be of about 67 burners, and whose estimated value for the entire horizon would reach, according to what has been heretofore said, to 24,120 burners.

The inherent expenses of this sort of apparatus may be set down at 13,698 francs, as follows:

Twenty-four lamps and reflectors	1608. 00 *fr.*
Armature, lantern, different kinds of supplies, transportation, and placing as above stated	12090. 00
Total	13698. 00

From which I = 684.90 *frs.*

Let us admit, that the annual expenses of maintenance will not differ from the preceding one, except in the consumption of oil, wicks, and chimneys. The attendance upon the apparatus will be doubtless a little more expensive, but that element may be disregarded; there is no such light on our coast, and it is not desired to place any figures in the calculations which are not entirely reliable; the expense then may be estimated at 10,038.62 francs, as follows:

Expense of oil, 24 × 0.050 *kg.* × 4000 + 262 *kg.* = 5062 *kg.*, at 1.51 *fr.*	7643. 62 *fr.*
Salaries of two keepers as above	1575. 00
Wicks, chimneys, &c.	560. 00
Care of apparatus, &c	260. 00
Total	10038. 62

Useful effect: $\frac{L}{I+D} = \frac{24120}{684.90 + 10038.62} = 2.25.$

Cost of the unity of light: $\frac{I+D}{L} = 0.445$ *fr.*

Relative useful effect of the two apparatus: $\frac{7.62}{2.25} = 3.39.$

If, as it frequently happens, the apparatus is required to illuminate only three-fourths of the horizon, this difference will not be so great, because no account can be taken of the luminous rays directed towards the land, and in that case the expense of the catoptric apparatus will be reduced in a greater proportion than in the others. The following figures would then be correct, which are sufficiently easily controlled, to allow of being stated without recurring to the elements:

Interest of cost of the lens apparatus........... I = 1000. 75 *fr.*
Expense of maintenance of the same........... D = 3139. 90

Useful effect: $\frac{L}{I+D} = \frac{24300}{1000.75 + 3139.90} = 5.87.$

Interest of cost of catoptric apparatus.......... I = 664. 80
Expense of maintenance of the same........... D = 7987. 72

Useful effect: $\frac{L}{I+D} = \frac{18090}{664.80 + 7987.72} = 2.09.$

Relative useful effect of the two apparatus: $\frac{5.87}{2.09} = 2.81.$

APPARATUS OF THE TWO LARGEST ORDERS.

To spread around the entire horizon, with a catoptric apparatus, a quantity of light comparable to that which would be produced by a fixed lens-light apparatus of the second order, it would be necessary to have one hundred reflectors of 0. 59*m.*, consuming 50 grammes of oil per hour, or of sixty reflectors of 0. 59*m.*, consuming 60 grammes. The luminous intensity of the lens apparatus being 335 burners; that of the reflector apparatus reaches to 279 burners in the first case, and varies in the second from 350 to 352 burners. The hourly consumption of oil by the two apparatus would be, respectively, 500, 5,000, and 3,600 grammes.

Besides, the placing and attendance of the catoptric apparatus of this description would present such difficulties to be overcome that none have ever been constructed, and it therefore appears to be useless to push the comparison further.

Should it be a question of a light of the first order, it would be found that, while the lens apparatus consuming 760 grammes per hour sends upon the entire horizon 630 burners, sixty reflectors of 0. 85*m.*, whose consumption reaches to 3,600 grammes, would only give an intensity varying from 550 to 630 burners.

But a similar apparatus would be much less allowable still than those already spoken of, of the second order, and consequently there is no occasion to say more in regard to these.

It is necessary, however, to add—to point out that which is true and to omit nothing having an important bearing on the subject—that if it should become necessary not to illuminate the entire horizon, as has been discussed, but a small angular space, the catoptric system will at once lose its want of power and its superiority in an economical point of view. Thus, let us suppose that the luminous rays only are to be distributed in an angle of 45°, it will require but eight reflectors of 0.85*m.*, with lamps of 1.60 *b.*, to have about the equivalent of an ordinary lens apparatus of the first order; for, as has been already said, the dispositions employed to collect, in these last apparatus, the divergent rays towards the dead angle does not exercise a very great influence upon the augmentation of the range. The consumption of oil of the catoptric apparatus will diminish then to 480 grammes, while it had been 760 grammes with the lens. The expenses of first establishing and of maintaining would be, besides, about the same in both systems. Doubtless it would not be difficult to conceive an arrangement of lenses better suited for a case like this than that which has been adopted, in case of a horizon exceeding one-half of the circumference; but it is easily conceived how inconvenient it would be, practically, to introduce a new type for each exceptional circumstance which might present itself. The only conclusion to arrive at, from what has preceded, is conformable to that which has been announced when the question of catoptric apparatus has been under consideration, and that is, that it recommends itself alone for illuminating very restricted angular spaces.

From what has been said of lights of the two larger orders, required to illuminate not less than the half of the horizon, the comparison between the two systems can only be made with the eclipse-light apparatus. We will limit ourselves to a single example, omitting all unnecessary details, except such as are required to put the question beyond all doubt.

CALCULATION FOR A LIGHT OF THE FIRST ORDER OF ECLIPSES EVERY MINUTE.

Lens Apparatus.

First establishing:

Apparatus, including the armature	37940. 00 *fr.*
Three mechanical lamps	2100. 00
Revolving machine	3200. 00
Different kinds of fixtures	900. 00
Lantern, including glazing and lightning conductor	20400. 00
Transportation and placing apparatus	3900. 00
Total	68440. 00

From which, following the notation hitherto adopted, I = 3422 *fr.*

Annual maintenance:

Oil, 3,205 kilogrammes, at 1. 51 *fr*	4830. 55 *fr.*
Salaries and fuel of three keepers	2525. 00
Wicks, chimneys, and different supplies	219. 00
Care of apparatus, &c., repairs, &c	390. 00
Total	7973. 55

The quantity of light expanded upon the horizon may be represented by 630 *b.* × 360 = 226,800 *b.*, which is the same whether the apparatus be revolving or fixed.

The catoptric apparatus, to be compared to the lens apparatus, must be composed of twenty-four reflectors of 0.85*m.*, each illuminated by a lamp of double wick, consuming 175 grammes of oil per hour, and divided in four groups of six lamps and reflectors each. The maximum of the flash will reach to 4,560 burners, while it will reach 5,075 with the lenses. The revolving machinery must be doubly as quick to produce the same intervals between the luminous appearances.

The expenses may be estimated as follows:

24 reflectors fitted with their lamps, at 865 *frs*	20760. 00 *fr.*
Armature	6300. 00
Revolving machine	3200. 00
3 spare reflectors	2595. 00
Fixtures, lantern, transportation, and putting up as above	25200. 00
Total	58055. 00

Annual maintenance:

Oil, 0.175 *kg.* × 24 × 4000 + 550 *kg.* = 17,350 *kg.*, at 1.51 *fr.*	26198.50 *fr.*
Salaries and fuel of three keepers	2525.00
Wicks, chimneys, and different supplies	2688.00
Different articles, the same figures as above, although too small here	390.00
Total	31801.50

From which I = 2,902.75 *fr.*, and D = 31, 801.50 *fr.*

The quantity of light conveyed to the horizon by one of these reflectors may be represented by the figures, 7,429 burners, which has been obtained by adding the mean luminous intensities of each of the degrees illuminated. That of the entire apparatus will have for expression L = 178,296 burners.

We shall then have the lens apparatus:

Useful effect $\frac{L}{I+D} = \frac{226,800}{3422 + 7973.55} = 19.90.$

Cost of the unity of light: $\frac{I+D}{L} = 0.050\,fr.$

And for the catoptric apparatus:

Useful effect: $\frac{L}{I+D} = \frac{178,296}{2902.75 + 31801.50} = 5.14.$

Cost of the unity of light: $\frac{I+D}{L} = 0.195\,fr.$

The first of these apparatus is then nearly four times more economical than the second. It is thus seen that the merit of the lens apparatus is much greater as it increases in power.

It is also to be remarked that the attendance upon twenty-four double-wick lamps would be exceedingly hard upon one man, and that it has never been performed with such an apparatus.

The most powerful eclipse catoptric apparatus which has been adopted in France is not composed of more than four reflectors of 0.85*m.* in a group, illuminated by lamps with a single wick. The intensity of their flashes does not exceed 2,700 burners, and it was, consequently, greatly inferior to those of the light-houses fitted with lens of the two larger orders, with which they were compared. At the light-house at Ailly, near Dieppe, the reflectors are twelve, disposed in groups of three, and the maximum intensity of the flashes was 1,650 burners; that is to say, little superior to that of an annular panel, complete, of the third order, embracing the eighth of the circumference, which gives 1,266 burners in the axis. It is, doubtless, unnecessary to insist longer with the view to make the merits of the new system fully appreciated. It is proper, however, to add to that which has been said already in regard to the superiority of the lens apparatus, that the attendance upon the lenses is much easier for the keepers, and consequently more sure and reliable than with the reflectors, as regards the economy of the luminous ray s

IV.—COLORED LIGHTS.

In pointing out the different characteristic distinctions given to the lights on the coasts of France, we have said that, after long hesitations, the Lights Commission (Commission des Phares) had allowed some of the lights to be distinguished by color, since it was established by satisfactory experiments that color did not cause the effect upon the ranges, which it was supposed up to that time was attributable to it.

Some observations made upon red lights have put the engineers of the lighting service on the right track in this regard. One of them was often surprised at the brilliancy which these lights presented at long distances, and it was asked if the action which produced a red light upon the retina would not diminish in a less degree than that of the white light, in proportion as the distance increases.*

It is known that, in clothes, paintings, glass, it is almost always the red color which strikes the sight the most vividly, and it is known also, that the blue and green, complimentaries of the orange and of red, afford to weak eyes a kind of relief, while the red produces upon them an impression almost painful, and, at the same time, to have for that organ fatal results, if prolonged beyond a certain limit.

The first condition to make of the experiments, for solving, if not rigorously, at least with a sufficiently close approximation, the problem which is presented, was to compare the power of lights of different colors, and to see if they are of the same intensity, or rather if they are equivalent as to visibility. But, in placing before a photometer, arranged as has been said before, two lights, one red, the other white, and in observing the two illuminated bands upon the screen, it is proved that, according as one of the lights is brought nearer, or moved further off from the instrument, the illuminated band, which corresponds to it, appears sometimes more and sometimes less brilliant than the near one, or, in other words, is sometimes more and sometimes less visible than the latter. Whatever may be the difference of coloration, a great nicety or sharpness may be given to that sensation of inequality between the two bands, in moving away properly one of the lights to be compared.

It is conceivable, then, that a certain practice of the experiments of this sort, and some groping, permits the restricting more and more the limits on the side of which there is certain inequality, and to arrive at a determination thus, in an approximative manner, of the photometric distances corresponding to equality. The appreciations of one observer differ sufficiently little, to allow the accordance of a certain scientific value to the means deduced from a great number of measurements; but all the organs are not affected in the same way by color, the judgments of different persons may be dissimilar, as will be seen further on.

That granted, the photometric experiments, although made necessarily at short distances, show that the law which obtains as to the decrease of visibility of colored lights, is not that of the square of the distances, which belongs to the white light. For the red, for example, if the observer placed near the photometer has established the equality between the two bands in separating properly the lights, and if it comes then further off, the red band will appear more brilliant than the white, and the difference will be much more marked, as it is further from the instrument. If it is desired to maintain the equality, it will become necessary to bring back the white light in proportion as it is moved

* A memoir has been presented, in 1858, to the Academy of Sciences by Monsieur the Engineer Degrand and myself.

further from the photometer. The reverse takes place when the color is green or blue; the comparative value of the colored light diminishes as the distance increases. Numerous experiments have put these phenomena beyond doubt; some of them will be given.

It is known that color is obtained by placing colored glass before the the lamp, or by surrounding the flame by a colored chimney. Both systems are employed in our lights, but recourse was had only to the first in the experiments referred to. The red color is produced by the salts of copper, silver, or gold, and the shades which correspond to them are, respectively, red with a deep purple tint, orange red more or less intense, and the rose red. The first of these colors is the most marked, and appears to absorb the most of the luminous rays, when observed at a short distance; the last possesses the opposite properties. The tones above all of those of red, from copper and from silver, vary otherwise, between sufficiently extended limits. Observations have been made by many persons who were successively placed at different distances from the photometer. The light taken for unity has been, as ordinarily, that of a carcel lamp consuming 40 grammes of oil per hour; but colored glass was also placed before lights of greater inten sity, so as to have the colors sufficiently bright upon the photometer. The intensities of these last flames have been otherwise very exactly appreciated by the observations made before the interposition of the colored glass. These glasses were placed at 0.30*m.* in front of the flames, and the photometer was 5 metres distant.

The following table shows the results of the experiments; the observed luminous intensities are expressed in the same way as of those which had given the same light not colored:

No. of observation.	Color.	Intensity of the flame.	No. of observation.	Value of the colored light, observed at a distance from photometer of—					Mean value, λ				
				0.20*m.*	2*m.*	4*m.*	6*m.*	8*m.*	0.20*m.*	2*m.*	4*m.*	6*m.*	8*m.*
		Brns.											
1	Red of gold...	23	1	0.272	0.396	0.472	0.518	0.571	0.262	0.382	0.482	0.555	0.614
			2	0.229	0.345	0.402	0.460	0.500					
			3	0.249	0.404	0.591	0.649	0.790					
			4	0.298	0.384	0.462	0.592	0.596					
2	Red of silver, ordinary....	21	1	0.124	0.174	0.270	0.350	0.439	0.191	0.250	0.325	0.404	0.413
			2	0.232	0.304	0.352	0.382	0.385					
			3	0.187	0.251	0.336	0.472*	0.451*					
			4	0.219	0.271	0.341	0.411*	0.376*					
3	Red of silver, very deep...	22	1	0.080	0.133	0.192	0.219	0.238	0.087	0.127	0.194	0.241	0.262
			2	0.094	0.096	0.187	0.207	0.249					
			3	0.094	0.163	0.227	0.347	0.362					
			4	0.082	0.116	0.169	0.190	0.200					

* The figures marked with an asterisk show anomalies and indicate an accidental and sudden modification in the flash of the flame.

The observations upon the green and the blue cannot be relied upon, the first beyond six metres, the second beyond two metres, because the colored belts were not very apparent.

Results of experiments—Continued.

No. of observation.	Color.	Intensity of the flame.	No. of observation.	Value of the colored light, observed at a distance from photometer of—					Mean value, λ				
				0.20*m*.	2*m*.	4*m*.	6*m*.	8*m*.	0.20*m*.	2*m*.	4*m*.	6*m*.	8*m*.
		Brns.											
4	Red of copper, ordinary	23	1	0.055	0.077	0.088	0.104	0.129	0.049	0.074	0.093	0.119	0.149
			2	0.044	0.063	0.083	0.133	0.191					
			3	0.052	0.086	0.114	0.148	0.183					
			4	0.044	0.071	0.086	0.089	0.093					
5	Red of copper, very deep	5.4	1	0.015	0.034	0.056	0.069	0.115	0.019	0.044	0.068	0.098	0.131
			2	0.015	0.051	0.075	0.107	0.144					
			3	0.022	0.048	0.070	0.102	0.118					
			4	0.024	0.042	0.071	0.115	0.147					
6	Green, ordinary	22	1	0.057	0.048	0.043	0.037	....	0.073	0.062	0.056	0.048	....
			2	0.071	0.053	0.048	0.041	....					
			3	0.080	0.076	0.064	0.062	....					
			4	0.084	0.072	0.070	0.053	....					
7	Green, deeper	4.5	1	0.040	0.034	0.030	0.028	....	0.049	0.038	0.033	0.030	....
			2	0.054	0.041	0.035	0.033	....					
			3	0.054	0.039	0.033	0.030	....					
8	Blue	14	1	0.015	0.012	....	....	....	0.015	0.012	....	....	....
			2	0.015	0.011	....	....	....					
			3	0.015	0.012	....	....	....					
			4	0.013	0.012	....	....	....					

The figures may appear to be too greatly multiplied; but they relate to phenomena which have not been before signalized, and are of great importance to maritime illumination. It has been considered necessary to show what degree of confidence to accord to the observations, and to make known that, if they are subject to differences sufficiently marked, they nevertheless conduce to the same general conclusion.

According to the mean values of the preceding table, the comparative intensities of the different colored lights have varied, as shown, as follows, for the observations made at the different distances from the photometer:

Color.		Report of intensities.		
		From 0.20*m*. to 2 metres.	From 0.20*m*. to 6 metres.	From 0.20*m*. to 8 metres.
Red	Gold	$\frac{382}{262} = 1.46$	$\frac{355}{262} = 2.12$	$\frac{614}{262} = 2.34$
	Silver, ordinary	$\frac{250}{191} = 1.31$	$\frac{404}{191} = 2.11$	$\frac{413}{191} = 2.16$
	Silver, very deep color	$\frac{127}{87} = 1.46$	$\frac{241}{87} = 2.77$	$\frac{262}{87} = 3.01$
	Copper, ordinary	$\frac{74}{49} = 1.51$	$\frac{119}{49} = 2.43$	$\frac{149}{49} = 3.04$
	Copper, very deep color	$\frac{44}{19} = 2.32$	$\frac{98}{19} = 5.16$	$\frac{131}{19} = 6.89$
Green	Ordinary	$\frac{62}{73} = 0.85$	$\frac{48}{73} = 0.68$	....
	Deeper color	$\frac{38}{49} = 0.77$	$\frac{30}{49} = 0.61$	....
Blue		$\frac{12}{15} = 0.80$	....	....

It will be remarked, that in the red lights the greater part of the reports are much higher as the color is intense, and that the copper red, which absorbs most of the light at short distances, is that which gains the most in proportion as it is observed further off. Experiments made with more powerful apparatus, seen at the distance of several kilometres, have equally shown, as will be soon seen, that it ends by being longer visible than the silver red.

The Figure 23, following this, represents, in a manner perhaps more striking than is shown by figures, the results arrived at in the last

FIG. 23.

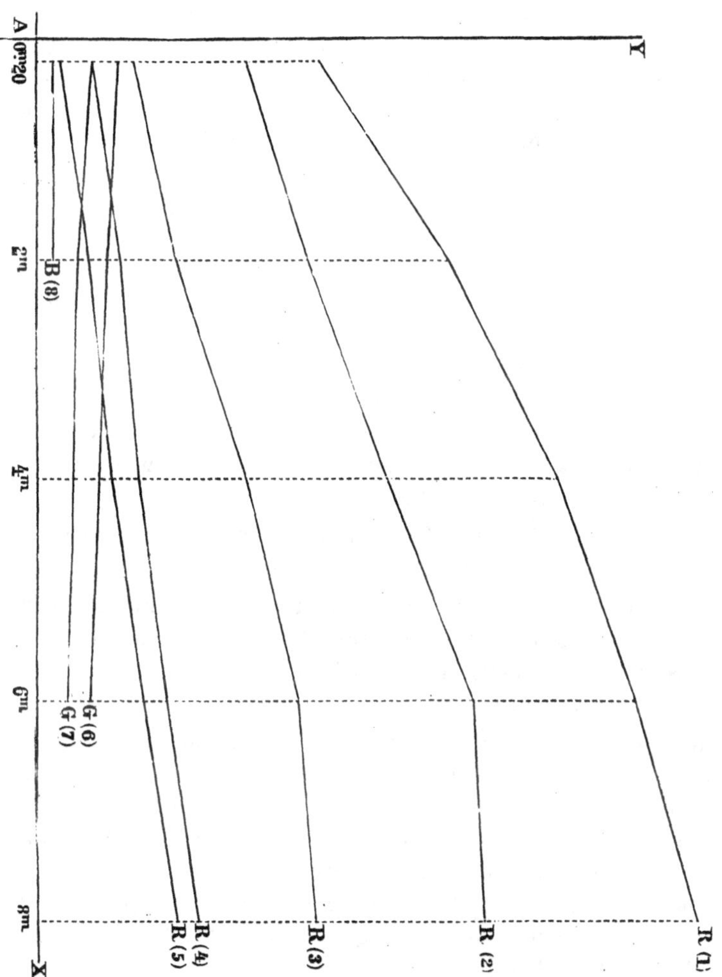

column of the first of these tables. It has been constructed by carrying the distances of the observer to the photometer upon the axis of the abscissæ, on a scale of 0.015*m.* per meter, and the luminous intensities on the axis of the ordinates, or 0. 15*m.* expresses the value of the uncolored light.

The broken line 1 is that of the gold red; the lines 2 and 3 those of the silver red; the lines 4 and 5 belong to the copper red; and the lines 6 and 7 are green. The blue, only having been observed twice, is represented by a right line, (8.)

In all the experiments it was sought, as far as possible, to guard against the influence which arises from accidental colors, and care was always taken to manage the photometer in such a way as to separate the white band from the colored one, by a black band of sufficient extent to prevent that source of error, which had given a green tint to the white when placed by the side of the red, or a red tint in the experiments upon green. The black band should produce, it is true, a contrast; but the white does not feel it less than the colored bands, and the effect was, otherwise, independent of the position of the observer.

Other experiments, made at greater distances, seemed to possess a greater value in a practical point of view.

In the first, five flames have been regulated in such a way, that, four of them being covered with red glass of the copper, silver, or gold, they all appeared to be of the same intensity to the photometer observed at 0.80*m.* distant. That intensity had been fixed at 0.005*m.* of the carcel burner, so that it might reach the limits of the ranges without going outside of the circuit of the Champ de Mars, in which the experiments were made. The sky was clear, the night still, and the observers, to the number of four, have reported as follows:

1. At a distance of about 500 metres, the white light ceased to be seen, whilst the red light, except that of the gold, was still bright.

2. At 750 metres, the same lights remained visible, but the red distinction was not distinct, except of the light which had been covered by a glass of deep copper-red color, whose absorption had been estimated at $\frac{99}{100}$ of the white light.

Another series of experiments was made with more powerful lights of parabolic reflectors of 0.29*m.* of opening, illuminated by lamps of an intensity equal to 1.30 *b.*, and giving consequently in their axes flashes whose intensity may be estimated perhaps at 60 burners for the white light. Before two of them copper-red panes of glass of different shades were placed, and before another a silver-red pane of glass. Two white reflectors have been brought back by uncolored panes, or of stone color or Spanish white, to present the same intensity at a short distance as the colored reflectors. The lights were too intense, even to the limits of their range. The observations were not carried beyond 3,300 metres; but the intensity of the red lights was always found to be, as compared to the white lights, apparently increasing with the distance.

At 800 metres, the five lights presented sensibly the same intensity; at 1,400 metres, there was a difference very appreciable in favor of the red lights; at 3,300 metres, these last, and especially those of the copper, exceeded greatly the others.

Two reflectors alike, the one covered with a copper-red glass, the other white, have been observed at that same distance of 3,300 metres. The report of their intensities, measured at a short distance, was $\frac{1}{1.20}$, and yet the first appeared more brilliant than the second.

Of analogous experiments made with green and blue, results diametrically opposite to the preceding were obtained.

All the colors lose their character when the limit of their range is approached, and end by being no longer appreciable; but that effect is much more marked with the green and blue than the red, and with the gold-red than the others, and, above all, with the copper red.

It is essential to add that all the experiments have been made during a clear and transparent atmosphere, so that the property of some fogs to give lights a red color has been without sensible action upon the phenomena. The white lights remain uncolored to the limits of their ranges. During the fogs referred to, the red are still more superior to the others, for they have little effect upon them, while they only allow the red rays of the white lights to pass, and diminish the green lights rapidly after having brought them back to white. On this subject the following experiment may be cited: Five reflectors, producing about 60 burners of white light in the axis, have been observed during fog. The light of the first was white, that of the second colored gold red, that of the third copper red, that of the fourth green, and that ot the last blue. The white light and the red light ceased to be seen at the distance of 1,600 metres; the color of gold red was distinguished with difficulty at 1,500 metres, whilst that of the copper-red light was sufficiently well marked. The green light disappeared at 1,000 metres and the blue light at 530 metres.

Finally, the observations made at long distances upon the red-colored lights in light-houses lead to the same conclusions as those of which account is about to be given, and in recurring to the subject may recall that which has already been said in regard to the light at Pontaillac.

It has been admitted, consequently, in the light service, that the red color, by a glass of copper-red color of suitable shade, will not reduce the intensity of the white light more than a quantity comprised between one-half and two-thirds, or in other words, that to obtain a red light and a white light of the same range in ordinary states of the atmosphere, it will be sufficient to allow to the first two to three times more of white rays than to the second. There is doubtless not much precision in this rule, but it may be said that the subject does not admit of it. It is upon this basis that apparatus are established in which the red beams alternate with white ones.

Thus, the apparatus of the first order, represented by the Figures 5 and 6 of the Plate 5, produces a light of eclipses in every twenty seconds, in which a red flash alternates with a white flash, and its cupola has been so arranged that all the luminous rays which it sends out are added to those which come from the colored panels of the drum and the lower rings.

The apparatus of the third order, Figures 7, 8, and 9 of the same plate, presents a fixed light, which is produced by the greater part of the dioptric drum, as well as by the catadioptric rings below, and this light is varied by alternate red and green flashes every twenty seconds, produced by annular panels, which are dioptric in the lower part and catadioptric above. In white lights the fixed light is equivalent to 60 burners, and each of the pannels will give in the axis of flash of 420 burners, which is reduced to about 150 burners at 2° on each side. The colored flashes are seen a little further than the white light, and those which are green are seen at a less distance than the others, especially during fogs.

FIG. 24.

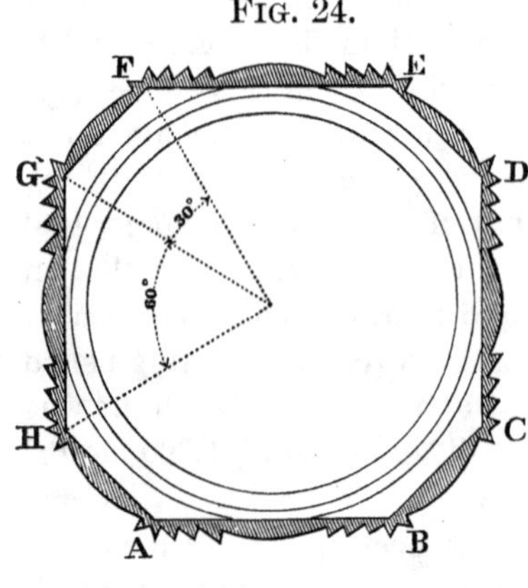

The sketch opposite represents the plan of an apparatus equal to the third order, whose dispositions in general come near the preceding, but which is designed for a fixed light varied by flashes every half minute, alternately red and white, without intervening eclipses. The large sides A B, C D, E F, G H, of the polygon, which forms the base of the movable part, belong to the panels which are required to produce the red rays; the angular spaces which they embrace are double of those which correspond to the white panels. When there is no fog, the range of the white flashes is a little greater than the others.

MODE OF COLORING.

In the fixed lights the flame is covered by a colored chimney. In the eclipse-light apparatus sheets of colored glass are placed on one side or the other, opposite the lenses which are to produce the colored flashes. They are mounted upon the bronze frames so as to be opened to allow dusting and cleaning of the glass itself, and also of the lenses.

V.—TYPES OF APPARATUS.

The disposition of the illuminating apparatus varies according to the conditions to be satisfied. We shall limit ourselves here to giving the principal actual types of the apparatus most in use upon the coasts of France, or which present the greatest degree of interest.

1. APPARATUS OF THE FIRST-ORDER FIXED LIGHT.

The Figures 1 and 2 of Plate 5 represent the plan and elevation of that apparatus;* its section is shown by Figure 1 of Plate 6, to the right. The Figure 2 of the same plate shows the elevation of one of its panels, which embraces an eighth of the circumference, and comprises eighteen catadioptric rings above the dioptric drum and eight below it. The fourth of the horizontal section of the apparatus occupies the angle C of the Figure 1 of Plate 4. The plan of the lamp is represented in *d* upon that last figure.

Intensity of the apparatus .... 630 burners.
Range in ordinary states of the atmosphere ....20. 2 miles.

The Figures 1 of Plate 1 represent the distribution, the intensity, and the range of the luminous rays produced by an apparatus of this sort.

2. APPARATUS OF THE FIRST-ORDER FIXED LIGHT, VARIED BY FLASHES EVERY FOUR MINUTES.

This apparatus does not differ from the preceding one but in having three vertical element lenses at equal distances revolving around the drum, which they encircle through their entire height. They each subtend an angle of 34° 12′, and they collect into beams the luminous rays already refracted by the cylindrical lens. The flashes which they produce are preceded and followed by eclipses of less duration than those of other revolving lights. These eclipses are, however, not total, except at great distances, since nothing obstructs the way of the rays sent out through the catadioptric rings. After the fixed light produced by the entire apparatus, comes a dimness very well marked, which constitutes a total eclipse beyond the distance of 16. 2 miles under ordinary states of the atmosphere, and whose duration is about twenty seconds at a short distance; then presents a very brilliant flash, which is suc-

* Plate 3 gives, upon a large scale, the different lenticular profiles actually in use.

ceeded by an eclipse similar to the preceding one, and followed by the fixed light.

The Figures 5 of the Plate 1 represent the distribution, intensity, and form of the luminous beams answering to these different conditions of the light.

The left side of the Figure 1 of the Plate 6 shows a section of the apparatus taken through the axis of one of the vertical element lenses, and the Figure 3 is an elevation of one of these lenses. The fourth of the horizontal section of the same apparatus occupies the angle B of the Figure 1 of Plate 4, where, at *c*, the revolving machine is shown.

Thus, as has been said in treating of the general dispositions of the illuminating apparatus, recourse is only had to vertical element lenses but for lights having a dead angle of 45° or less. For those which are required to illuminate the entire horizon, annular lenses are introduced in the drum, and the entire system receives the movement of rotation, as shown by the small apparatus of Plate 11.

Habitual intensity of the fixed light, 630 burners; range, 20. 2 miles.

Intensity of the fixed light during the eclipses, 190 burners; range, 16. 2 miles.

Intensity of the flash, 4,000 burners; range, 27. 0 miles.

3. APPARATUS OF THE FIRST-ORDER ECLIPSE LIGHT, ONCE EVERY MINUTE, (PROLONGED FLASHES.)

The Figures 3 and 4 of Plate 5 give the plan and elevation of that apparatus, the half of the horizontal section of which is represented on the left side of Figure 1 of Plate 4. The Figure 1 of Plate 7 gives, to the left, a section taken, following the axis of one of the panels of the drum, and to the right, a section directed through one of the angles of the polygon. The Figure 2 of the same plate, is the elevation of one of the panels of the apparatus. The annular catadioptric lens shows in horizontal projection an angle of 4° with that of the drum to which it is attached, in a way to increase the duration of the flash, and the lower catadioptric rings constitute the fixed light. The drum and the catadioptric crown only are put in motion by the revolving machinery. That machine is seen in elevation and section, and indicated at *c* on the plan.

The Figures 2 of the Plate 1 represent the distribution, intensity, and the form of the luminous beams of that apparatus.

Intensity of the flashes, 5,075 burners; range, 27.9 miles.

Intensity of the fixed light between the flashes, 60 burners; range, 12.7 miles.

4. APPARATUS OF THE FIRST-ORDER OF ECLIPSES, ONCE EVERY THIRTY SECONDS, (PROLONGED FLASHES.)

This apparatus differs from the preceding one, in so far that the regular polygon which forms its base is composed of sixteen sides instead of eight. The Figure 3 of the Plate 7 represents one of its faces, and the Figure 3 of Plate 1 shows its effect.

Intensity of the flashes, 2,525 burners; range, 25.2 miles.

Intensity of the fixed light between the flashes, 60 burners; range, 12.7 miles.

5. APPARATUS OF THE FIRST-ORDER OF ECLIPSES, ONCE IN EVERY TWENTY SECONDS AND BELOW.

The number of sides of the polygon of this apparatus is twenty-four, and, the luminous appearances being in very quick succession, it has not been judged necessary to prolong the duration of the flashes, nor to preserve a fixed light between the intervals; each dioptric panel has two catadioptric annular panels placed upon the same axis with it. The Figure 4 of Plate 7 gives the elevation of one of the faces of the apparatus, which turn entirely around. The armature, the lower catadioptric panels, and the drum, are disposed, as may be seen by the Figure 6 of the Plate 5. In the revolving apparatus, which is to be described, the lower zone is fixed, which allows entrance to the interior, by a passage through an open ring, which occurs when it is not necessary to illuminate the entire horizon, or when the fixed light in a space of 45° may be dispensed with; but here, the movement of rotation being given to the whole apparatus, it becomes necessary to have recourse to a special arrangement, so that the keeper may reach the lamp without arresting the revolutions of the apparatus. The place of entrance has been lowered for that purpose; the uprights which rest upon the chariot are brought together in such a way as not to obstruct the passage around the foot of the apparatus; they are only six in number, and three steps lead to the landing on the service table.

The Figures 4 of Plate 1 point out the distribution, and show the intensity and form of the luminous beams emanating from an apparatus of this sort. The upper figure shows, to the left, the flashes which succeed each other every twenty seconds, and, to the right, flashes with only three seconds between them.

Intensity of the flashes, 2,450 burners; range, 25. 1 miles.

6. APPARATUS OF THE FIRST ORDER OF ECLIPSES, OF TWENTY SECONDS' INTERVALS AND BELOW, IN WHICH A RED FLASH ALTERNATES WITH A WHITE ONE.

This apparatus is represented in plan and elevation by the Figures 5 and 6 of Plate 5. The panels of the lower zone and of the drum are twenty-four in number, and there are but twelve in the upper zone. Two of the first produce white flashes; and to constitute red flashes, one of the last is added to them. The color is given by pieces of plane glass placed in the interior of the apparatus, before the lenses. Those of the two first zones are vertical, the others are inclined, and form a kind of pyramidal roof. All are fitted in light bronze frames, which open with hinge joints.

Intensity of the white flashes, 1,825 burners; range, 24 miles.

Intensity of the three superposed panels, if not fitted with red glass, 3,075 burners.

By recalling what has been said about the absorption of the luminous rays by color, it may be judged from these figures that, under ordinary circumstances of atmosphere, the white flashes ought to have a little greater range than the red ones.

In an apparatus of this description, which illuminates the light-house at the Point of Créac'h, (Isle of Ouessant,) two white flashes alternate with one red. The upper cupola is divided then into eight panels, and the intensity of the colored flashes would reach 3,725 burners if they were white. About double the quantity of luminous rays is employed for the red flashes as for the others, from which it follows that the range of the two kinds of beams is about the same. This last characteristic is, under this aspect, preferable to the preceding.

The intensity of the red flashes of this last, might, it is true, be augmented by applying to the first zone the same disposition as to the third; but that would have been at the expense of the white flashes, whose intensities were found to be insufficient.

7. APPARATUS OF THE SECOND-ORDER FIXED LIGHT.

This apparatus is similar to that of the first order, differing only in dimensions and the number of rings.

The half plan of this apparatus is represented by the part B of the Figure 2 of Plate 4; the half section is seen to the right upon the Figure 1 of Plate 8. The Figure 2 of the same plate gives the elevation of one of these panels which embraces one-sixth of the circumference.

Intensity of the light, 335 burners; range, 18 miles.

8. APPARATUS OF THE SECOND ORDER OF ECLIPSES.

The apparatus of the second order of eclipse lights are similar to those of the first order. The sides of the polygon are eight in number when the intervals are one minute, and twelve only when the flashes succeed each other every thirty seconds. The number of panels is not doubled as in the first order, to prevent too great a reduction of the intensity. The apparatus takes only six minutes to complete its entire revolution instead of eight minutes, and the duration of the flashes is reduced in like manner. These flashes are prolonged, as in the first order, by the panels of the cupola.

When the interval of the eclipses is twenty seconds and below, the number of panels is increased to twenty, the fixed light is suppressed, and all the lenses of a panel are placed upon the same axis.

In the apparatus of the second order, varied by flashes, the vertical element lenses always embrace an angular space of 43° 40′, and only cover the drum.

To the left of the Figure 2, Plate 4, and of Figure 1, Plate 8, is represented the half of the plan and half of the section of an apparatus of the second order, whose eclipses succeed each other every thirty seconds. The Figure 3 of this last plate gives the elevation of one of these panels.

The Figures 7 and 8 of Plate 1 represent, respectively, the distribution, intensity, and form of the luminous beams emanating from the apparatus of the second order—one of eclipses of thirty seconds, and the other a fixed light varied by flashes every three minutes.

Intensity of the flashes of an apparatus of the second order of eclipses.

Once every minute: 2,550 burners; range, 25. 3 miles.

Of thirty seconds: 1,675 burners; range, 23. 7 miles.

Of twenty seconds and under: 1,450 burners; range, 23. 2 miles.

Intensity of the fixed light between the flashes of the two first apparatus, 25 burners; range, 10. 3 miles.

Apparatus with vertical element lenses.

Intensity of the flashes, 2,700 burners; range, 25. 5 miles.

Intensity of the fixed light, 335 burners; range, 18. 0 miles.

Intensity of the fixed light during the eclipses, 95 burners; range, 14. 0 miles.

9. APPARATUS OF THE THIRD-ORDER FIXED LIGHT.

Half plan and half section of this apparatus are represented to the left of the Figure 3 of Plate 4, and of Figure 1 of Plate 9.

The Figure 2 of this last plate gives the elevation of one of these panels, which embraces a fifth of the circumference.

Intensity of the light, 90 burners; range, 13. 9 miles.

10. APPARATUS OF THE THIRD ORDER, VARIED BY FLASHES EVERY THREE MINUTES.

Half the plan and half the section of this apparatus is represented to the right of Figure 3, Plate 4, and of Figure 1, Plate 9. The Figure

3 of this last plate gives the elevation of one of the lenses of vertical elements, which embraces an angle of 44° 32′, and only covers the drum.

The Figures 12 of Plate 1 represent the distribution, intensity, and the form of the luminous beams of an apparatus of this sort.

Constant intensity of the fixed light, 90 burners; range, 13. 9 miles.

Intensity of the fixed light during the eclipses, 25 burners; range 10. 3 miles.

Intensity of the flash, 950 burners; range, 21. 6.

11. APPARATUS OF THE THIRD ORDER, VARIED BY FLASHES, WITHOUT ECLIPSES.

The arrangement which constitutes this new characteristic has been applied, for the first time, to the light of Walde, the lantern and apparatus of which are represented upon Plate 10. The lower half of the drum, and the catadioptric rings above and below, constitute a fixed light, which spreads its rays upon the entire horizon, except in the dead angle on the land side. The upper part of the drum is composed of twelve annular half lenses; they revolve and produce the flashes, which succeed each other at intervals of every twenty seconds. The apparatus is illuminated by a lamp with two wicks, consuming 175 grammes of oil per hour.

The cylindrical drum has only 0. 46*m.* of interior diameter.

Finally, to render this light more characteristic, the annular half lenses of the drum are covered with red glass, and embracing an angular space of 9°, which corresponds to the divergence of these lenses; bands of the same glass have been placed above and below in a way to color the fixed light, and to prevent the blending of the white rays with the others. The Figure 3 shows very neatly and clearly this arrangement.

This apparatus has been constructed, not like the preceding ones, of polished glass, but of glass run simply in moulds prepared with great care.

Intensity of the fixed light, 18 burners; range, 9. 4 miles.

Intensity of the uncolored flashes, 270 burners; range, 17. 3 miles.

The more important apparatus, which has not been spoken of yet, is treated in the same general way. One of them is represented in horizontal projection and in elevation by the Figures 7, 8, and 9 of Plate 5. The profile of its lenses is the same as has been adopted lately for third-order eclipse lights. The part which constitutes the fixed light is composed of the lower catadioptric rings, and of the cylindrical lens of the drum, including the first echelon which follows the joint ring; its height is 0. 80*m.* The movable part occupies the summit of the apparatus, and is formed of ten annular panels, which embrace all the upper catadioptric rings and the five upper echelons of the drum. The lenses are in part dioptric and in part catadioptric. They are covered outside by colored glass, forming a drum having a decagonal base, which turns with it. Each of the faces is extended downwards by a small glass band, as in the apparatus of Walde, and for the same reason.

The panels are colored alternately red and green, and the revolution is made in three minutes and twenty seconds.

The apparatus then produces a fixed white light, varied, at intervals of twenty seconds, by alternate red and green flashes. The duration of each of these flashes is about two seconds at long distances.

Intensity of the fixed light, 60 burners, range 12.7 miles.

The intensity of the flash, when it is not colored, reaches to 420 burners in the axis, and falls to about 150 burners at 2° on each side. Under ordinary states of the atmosphere, the colored flashes have a greater range than the fixed light; in foggy weather, the green flashes are soonest lost in leaving the light, as has already been stated when treating of colored lights.

It may be remarked that the revolving machinery is placed in the pedestal which supports the apparatus; that arrangement will be spoken of again, as the application of it has been multiplied lately.

If the colored glass is removed, there will be a fixed light, varied at intervals more or less close, by flashes, which will be neither preceded nor followed by eclipses.

The Figure 11 of Plate 1 exhibits an apparatus of this kind, in which the flashes are not colored.

12. APPARATUS OF THE THIRD ORDER OF ECLIPSES.

The apparatus of the third order of eclipses, once a minute or of thirty seconds, only differ in regard to dimensions from those of the second order of the same character; the drum is composed in first case of eight lenses, and of twelve in the second. It has not appeared to be necessary to give the drawings, which can be easily prepared according to the elements already furnished to the reader, and it will suffice to say that the Figure 10 of Plate 1 represents the distribution, the intensity, and the form of the luminous beams which emanate from an apparatus of that class of prolonged flashes whose eclipses succeed each other every thirty seconds.

Whenever the interval of the flashes come down to twenty seconds and lower, the drum has for its base a polygon of sixteen sides, the fixed light between the flashes is suppressed, and all the annular panels of each face are placed on the same axis, for the purpose of assuring to the flashes a suitable intensity.

Intensity of the flashes of a third-order eclipse apparatus.

Once every minute: 845 burners; range, 21. 2 miles.

Once every thirty seconds: 550 burners; range, 19. 7 miles.

Once every twenty seconds and less: 590 burners; range, 20. 0 miles.

Intensity of the fixed light between the flashes of the two first apparatus, 7 burners; range, 7. 2 miles.

13. APPARATUS OF THE THIRD ORDER, (SMALL MODEL.)

This name is given to apparatus of 0. 50*m.* diameter in the interior, illuminated by a double-wick lamp, which consumes 110 grammes of oil per hour.

The Figure 13 of Plate 1 represents an apparatus for a fixed light of this description.

Intensity, 30 burners; range, 10. 8 miles.

The Plate 11 represents one of these apparatus, giving a fixed light varied by flashes. In place of being produced by lenses of vertical elements passing in front of the drum, the flashes are produced by annular lenses, including all the catadioptric rings. The eclipses which separate the fixed light from the flashes are total.

In other apparatus of the same character, lenses of vertical elements, which only cover the drum and the lower catadioptric rings, are admitted. The Figures 10 and 11 of Plate 5 give the plan and elevation of an apparatus of this description, in which the flashes succeed each other at intervals of two or three minutes, according to the velocity of the revolving machinery.

The Figure 15 of Plate 1 renders an account of the effects of one of these apparatus, in which the movable lenses only cover the drum, and where the intervals which separate the flashes are extended to three minutes.

Eclipse apparatus of the same dimensions have been constructed. Some of them, composed of six annular panels, comprise the whole or a part of the height, and their flashes always succeed each other every minute. Others contain ten panels, and the intervals between their flashes descend to thirty seconds and less. The Figures 12 and 13 of Plate 5 give the plan and elevation of an apparatus of that order, in which the eclipses succeed each other every minute.

The upper catadioptric rings constitute a fixed light, which appears between the flashes which are produced by the annular lenses comprising the drum and the lower catadioptric rings.

The Figure 14 of Plate 1 represents the distribution, the intensity, and the form of the luminous beams emanating from an apparatus of the third order (small model) of eclipses, every twenty seconds, in which the fixed light is limited to the lower catadioptric rings. The intensity of the flashes reaches to 175 burners, and that of the fixed light to 2.5 burners.

Intensity of the flashes of an eclipse light, with fixed light produced by the upper catadioptric rings.

Once every minute: 275 burners; range, 17.4 miles.

Once every thirty seconds and less: 165 burners; range, 15.7 miles.

Intensity of the fixed light, 6 burners; range, 6.9 miles.

Intensity of the flashes of an apparatus of total eclipses, similar to that on Plate 11, 340 burners; range, 18.1 miles.

14. APPARATUS OF THE FOURTH ORDER.

The lens apparatus of the fourth order are of two principal dimensions; those of 0.375*m.*, the others of 0.30*m.* diameter in the interior. They are illuminated by single-wick lamps, whose diameter varies from 0.024*m.* (large burner) to 0.021*m.* (small burner) when colza oil is used. The Figures 1 and 2, 3 and 4, of Plate 12, represent two of these apparatus for fixed lights, illuminating three-fourths of the horizon, and fitted with constant-level lamps. Recourse is had to moderator lamps when it is necessary to illuminate the entire horizon.

There is nothing to prevent the establishing of eclipse lights upon these restricted dimensions, but there are none of them on the coast of France. The lights of short range are almost always placed in such a position that the navigators are interested in having them always visible, and as they are much less exposed than the others, to lead to mistakes. They only differ in color, and sometimes by the flashes succeeding each other every two, three, or four minutes.

The most of the apparatus of this order are actually illuminated by the oil of schiste or of petroleum, consuming 65 grammes per hour.

The Figures 16 and 17 of Plate 1 show the effects produced, the first by an apparatus of 0.375*m.* diameter for a fixed light, the second by an apparatus of the same dimensions, in which the flashes which succeed each other every two minutes are produced by vertical element lenses of the same height as the apparatus, and, consequently, accompanied by total eclipses.

The Figures 5 and 6 of Plate 12 represent a small apparatus for a fixed light of 0.30*m.* diameter, which is made of mould glass. It has no catadioptric rings, but the height of its drum has been carried to 0.40*m.* Placed in a small lantern designed to be hoisted upon a spar, it is necessary to have it very light.

The apparatus of this description do not admit of the use of the oil of schiste on account of the currents of air to which they are exposed, and their intensity does not exceed about six burners, but they are better under all circumstances than the sideral apparatus which they succeed.

One of the constructors, Mr. L. Sautter, constructs these apparatus in cut glass, which are somewhat better than the others.

The Figures 7 and 8 of the same plate give the elevation and section of an apparatus of mould glass designed for a range light. The rays which would diverge to the side of the land are brought back by a spherical reflector, the others are refracted by a large annular lens. Such of these last as would come in contact with the plane of the lens, under too open an angle, are divided first of all by a small conical lens.

The Figures 9 and 10 represent the elevation and the section of an apparatus of the same kind, which has been constructed in cut glass. It is composed equally of a reflector and an annular lens; but that lens is formed in part of dioptric and in part of catadioptric rings. It has more intensity and less divergence than the other.

Neither the one nor the other of these apparatus has come up to the expectations of their constructors; they possess less merit than the large reflectors of 0.95*m.* diameter. The drawings have only been reproduced to state the fact and to meet objections.

The Figures 11, 12, and 13 of Plate 12 give the plan, front elevation, and the lateral elevation of a single-sheet reflector or photophore of 0.29*m.* of opening, which is mounted on a pedestal and illuminated by a constant-level lamp fed by colza oil. These small apparatus, which are very economical, are usually placed upon a table in front of one of the windows of the light-keeper's house, and are frequently used for forming a range-light line.

Lastly, the Figures 14 and 15 represent a sideral apparatus, fitted in a movable lantern.

Apparatus of 0. 375*m. of fixed light.*

Lamp of large burner: intensity, 13 burners; range, 8. 6 miles.

Lamp with oil of schiste: intensity, 24 burners; range, 10. 2 miles.

Apparatus of 0. 30*m. fixed light.*

Lamp of small burner: intensity, 9 burners; range, 7. 8 miles.

Lamp with oil of schiste: intensity, 18 burners; range, 9. 4 miles.

Apparatus of 0. 375*m., varied by flashes, movable lenses covering only the drum.*

Lamp of large burner: intensity, fixed light, 13 burners; range, 8. 6 miles.

Lamp of large burner: intensity, flashes, 118 burners; range, 14. 7 miles.

Lamp of oil of schiste: intensity, fixed light, 24 burners; range, 10. 2 miles.

Lamp of oil of schiste: intensity, flashes, 221 burners; range, 16. 7 miles.

Movable apparatus for a fixed light of mould glass and small-burner lamp, (Figs. 5 and 6:) intensity, 6 burners, range, 6. 9 miles.

Range Lights:

Figs. 7 and 8, large-burner lamp: intensity, 200 burners; range 16. 4 miles.

Figs. 9 and 10, large-burner lamp: intensity, 300 burners; range, 17. 7 miles.

Figs. 11, 12, and 13, small-burner lamp: intensity, 60 burners; range, 12. 7 miles.

Sideral apparatus: lamp consuming 45 grammes of colza oil per hour, (Figs. 14 and 15:) intensity, 3. 5 burners; range, 5. 8 miles.

15. APPARATUS FOR LIGHT-VESSEL, FIXED LIGHT.

Plate 13 shows the drawings of an apparatus for a floating fixed light, placed in its lantern. As has been already stated, this apparatus is composed of ten reflectors of 0.29*m*. of opening, lighted each by a constant-level lamp, consuming 50 grammes of colza oil per hour, and whose burner is not placed in the focus of the paraboloid, for the reason that the luminous rays should not be too unequally distributed in the plane of the horizon. The curve *b b b* of Figure 9, page 50, shows the distribution of these rays. The maximum of intensity reaches to 38 burners, and the minimum to 18. The range is comprised between 11.4 and 9.4 miles.

Each lamp reposes upon a small chair of iron, to which it is attached by two clamps, and carries its reflector fixed in the same way. It is so arranged that the centre of gravity of the upper reservoir finds itself upon the same vertical as that of the lower cup when the reflector is in its normal position. That position—that is to say, the horizontality of the axis—is assured by means of a leaden weight placed under the reservoir. Each reflector is suspended in such a manner that it oscillates in every direction independently of the motion of the vessel; the chair which supports it turns upon two axes in the same plane, parallel to each other, normal to the paraboloid. The amplitude of the movement in each direction does not exceed 60°. It is indicated on the Figures 5 and 6 by the dotted lines.

The suspension rings of the ten lamps and reflectors are fixed upon a horizontal circle made of bronze, which move by means of rollers upon a fixed circle of the same material, whose section is in the form of armor plates. The lateral frictions are reduced by small horizontal rollers to the number of ten. The fixed circle is supported by four uprights, which constitute the fulcrum of the lantern around the mast. The movable circle is sustained during the night by a clutch, in such a position that each reflector is kept in the axis of one of the panels of the lantern.

This lantern is decagonal in shape. It is 1.44*m.* in diameter, between two opposite uprights, and 1 metre in height, exclusive of the cornice. Glazed in its upper part 0.46*m.* in height, it is closed everywhere else by sheets of copper, and in every alternate panel it is open below by a door of two sides. The dark panel panes open below; their frames slide in the lateral grooves arranged upon the uprights. By means of these doors, the interior sides of the panes of glass are cleaned; one pane is lowered for the purpose of lighting, to remove the reflectors, or to replace them and the lamps, &c.

The ventilation by means of ten ventilators, placed in the bottom of the lantern, whose movable part can be opened more or less; the disengagement of the products of the combuston is effected by means of chimneys in position, as shown by the section of Figure 2, in such a way that the external air cannot penetrate the lantern with sufficient force to cause the flames to become unsteady.

The lantern slides up and down the mast in attaching its four interior uprights to as many directing ledges, and two of these uprights carry jaws which embrace the corresponding ledges. That disposition is shown by the Figures 1, 2, 3, and 4. Two vertical rods of iron traverse the lantern, are sustained by a screw on the lower circle, and are fastened at their top by the suspension chain. The lantern is constructed entirely of bronze, except the panels, which are of copper.

The total weight of the apparatus and its lantern may be estimated at 830 kilogrammes.*

Fig. 1. Elevation of the lantern and apparatus.

Fig. 2. Section taken following the line A B of Figure 3.

Fig. 3. Plan taken at the height of the line C D of Figure 2.

Fig. 4. Plan taken at the height of the line E F of Figure 2.

Figs. 5, 6, and 7. Principal elevation, lateral elevation, and plan of a reflector and its lamp.

16. APPARATUS OF A FLOATING ECLIPSE LIGHT.

An apparatus for a floating eclipse light is represented on Plate 14. The reflectors are eight in number. They are 0.37*m.* of opening, and illuminated by constant-level lamps, consuming 60 grammes of colza oil per hour, and whose flames are placed in the focus of the parabola.

---

* 1 kilogramme = 2,206 pounds.

The maximum of intensity of the luminous beams emanating from one of these apparatus may be put down practically at 100 burners; the divergence in the horizontal plane is about 30°. The range in the axis is 14. 2 miles.

The lamps and reflectors are arranged similar to those described. The revolving movement is communicated to the circle which supports them by a large fixed-tooth wheel upon the upper surface of the circle. That wheel, whose teeth are turned towards the side of the mast, unites with a pinion placed at the summit of a vertical hollow iron shaft, which causes the revolutions of the machinery by the intermediary of a toothed wheel and another pinion. That machine is moved by a weight which descends with little friction between four iron directing guides. It is placed below the deck at the foot of the mast.

The revolving shaft is covered throughout its length above the deck by a half-cylinder of brass, which is fixed to a ledge nailed to the mast. Its foot carries a stem or point made of steel, which turns upon an agate set at the head in a glass which allows its elevation or depression by a small quantity.

Its length is divided into three or four parts, and its parts are reunited by boxes, which render them solid, so far as the rotation movement is concerned, but allows them to dilate or contract without arresting the revolutions, when it bends a little under the action of a storm. A small door opens in the cylindrical covering of the shaft in front of each of the expansion boxes.

Whenever the lantern is hoisted, its toothed wheel need not be fitted immediately with its pinion; that last wheel is then hoisted by the first, and is rested upon it by a spiral spring, which compels it to redescend from there by means of the movement of the machine, the teeth of each wheel being thus in their proper position. This spring is shown by Figure 6.

It is important to provide the means of keeping the lantern lower during bad weather than in good, which may be done in the following manner: A pinion similar to that at the summit is fixed half way up the shaft, and that last piece, as well as the large-toothed wheel of the apparatus, is maintained in a certain position whenever it may be necessary to raise or lower the lantern, in such a way that nothing opposes its passage, and it may be stopped at either of the pinions. The clutches are raised before the machinery is put in motion.

The lantern is the same in construction and arranged in the same manner as the preceding one, with the exception of the dimensions and the number of sides.

Fig. 1. Section of the lantern and of the mast taken along the line A B of the plan. The lantern is represented in the position which it occupies during the night, the directing shaft or rod, the revolving machine, and the motive weights are shown in elevation, and an alarm bell, *o*, is seen, which is sounded as soon as the motive weights come near the end of their course.

Fig. 2. Plan taken at the height of C D of Figure 1.

Fig. 3. Plan taken at the height of E F of Figure 1.

Figs. 4 and 5. Elevation and plan of the lower part of the directing shaft or rod.

Figs. 6 and 7. Elevation and plan of the summit of the same shaft or rod.

Figs. 8, 9, and 10. Elevation, section, and plan, showing the arrangement of one of the assemblage boxes.

17. REVOLVING MACHINE—ACCESSORY CONSTRUCTIONS.

Revolving machinery puts the movable parts of the apparatus in motion. They are moved by weights, and their number of revolutions is regulated by a flying pendulum. Always placed alongside of the apparatus, they are connected with it by a toothed wheel, so arranged as to be geared or thrown out of gear at will. The cord which suspends the motive weights passes through the vault or the floor which supports the illuminating apparatus in a groove fitted for that purpose, and the weights sent by a roller and pulleys descend in a vertical enclosure fitted on one side of the tower.

Some new apparatus have their revolving machinery placed in the foot of the armature, which has been enlarged in consequence. The Figure 9 of the Plate 5 offers an example of this sort of arrangement.

The weights are of about 75 kilogrammes in the revolving machine of first-order lights actually in use; it is muffled, and its estimated rate of speed is one metre per hour.

Armatures.

The armatures of the apparatus of the three largest orders are supported upon hollow cast-iron columns, which are screwed at their feet in the vault, and which are crowned by the table of the apparatus. That table, which was formerly of wood, is now of cast iron; it is upon it that the keeper stands when it becomes necessary to touch the lamp. The tables of the first order are fitted with drawers, in which different articles required in the service are kept.

The uprights of iron which unite the tie pieces start from the table; they rise to the entire height of the drum, and the circle in which they are assembled above serves as the point of support for the catadioptric panels of the crown. These panels are sustained in their positions by screws, and are surmounted by a cross bar which holds the pin of the centrage in the fixed apparatus, and carries in the revolving apparatus the horizontal rollers, which move around a vertical iron collar fixed to the lantern. In eclipse lights the whole or a part of the armature is movable, according to the arrangement of the apparatus.

The movement of rotation is operated upon a chariot of vertical rollers, which turn between the lower table of the movable apparatus and that which supports the capital of the cast-iron column. The horizontal rollers are introduced to reduce the friction. This latter table has been constructed heretofore in wrought or cast iron, and was not long in becoming worn by the wheel-work and the action of the rollers; at present it is constructed of steel, and the rollers of bronze. The wear rests especially upon these last works, which are easier to replace than the table, and are so arranged, besides, as to allow of their being renewed. The vertical rollers may be removed out or in; they are fitted for that purpose with movable washers, which surround their axes and are applied at will to either of their faces.

Lanterns.

The lanterns are polygonal. The table below shows their forms and their uniform dimensions:

Order of light.	Number of sides.	Interior diameter between the uprights.	Height of the glazing, including the ties.	Height of the cupola, including the ball.
1st	16	3.[illegible]0m.	2.32m.	2.53m.
2d	12	3.00	2.60	2.29
3d	10	2.50	1.90	1.88
4th	8	1.60	1.12	1.16

The uprights, the fastenings, and the arcs of the cupolas of the lanterns of the three largest orders are constructed of iron. The uprights are covered outside by a strip of bronze fastened by screws and pewter solder. The sills and fastening are of bronze. The cupola is formed of sheets of copper secured by small bolts, fitted with covered joints, which are directed according to the meridians and bolted after soldering in place.

The fourth-order lanterns are of such restricted dimensions that the cupolas are constructed of one single piece, and are simply fixed to the upper tie. Iron is not used in the construction of these small lanterns. The uprights are of bronze, as well as the ties.

Heretofore the uprights were planted in the masonry walls, forming the bed of the lantern. Now they are placed on the interior rim of the circle, and that plan has been found to give the advantage of augmenting the interior diameter of the sub-base, and the width of the small exterior platform upon which the keepers stand to clean the plate-glass of the lantern. The first system is always retained for the greater part of the lights, where, on account of a deficiency of space, it is necessary to reduce as much as possible the diameter of the tower.

The ventilation of the lantern is a most essential object, and many plans have been successively adopted with the view to render it as efficacious as possible. The object is twofold: to assist greatly in the consumption of the lamp, and to diminish the aqueous precipitations produced on the interior of the lantern glass, which has the effect of reducing more or less the brilliancy of the light.

A chimney, which is principally designed to carry off the products of combustion, and the air which the flame puts in motion, is fitted to the summit of the cupola. It is capped with a sphere pierced with holes at its lower part. In the lanterns of the three largest orders the air necessary for proper combustion comes through the hollow column designed for the descent of the lamp weights by the half opened ladder door, and often by the open ventilators in the masonry sub-base of the lantern, which are adjusted by registers. The longitudinal openings, which are opened or closed at will, are employed, besides, in the lower floors of the lantern, and above each of them. At the foot of the cupola is a small ventilating chimney which assists in expelling the hot air, and consequently in bringing in cold air.

The Plates 6, 7, 8, and 9 show these arrangements.

A large copper basin is suspended in each lantern above the top of the apparatus to catch the falling drops of water, whether of filtrations or precipitations upon the cupola, which might fall upon the flame or chimney. It is represented upon all of the sections of lanterns.

The glazing is done with panes of plate-glass of 0.008*m*. thickness. These panes are placed in the rabbets and kept in their positions by slats fixed by means of screws, as well upon the uprights as the traverses. Care must be taken to give about 0.002 of play all around the plate of glass to prevent, as far as possible, their rupture by the oscillations caused by tempests; they rest upon small pieces of lead, after which they are puttied all around.

Many panes of lantern glass have been broken, notwithstanding their thickness, by the shock of birds, such as ducks and geese, attracted by the brilliancy of the light. Nine of these panes of glass have been smashed in one night at the Cape Ferret light-house. At the Bréhat light-house a wild goose passed between two courses of mirrors, after having gone through the lantern pane, and fell upon the lamp. The lanterns of the lights which are most exposed to accidents of this sort, on account of their positions, are surrounded by fenders made of brass wire of 0.0012*m*. diameter, with meshes of about 0.08*m*. of openings. This causes a little weakening of the brilliancy of the lights. It is to be remarked, however, that the number of birds which have come in contact with the lanterns have so greatly decreased, from year to year, since the lights have been established, that probably the greater part of these fenders may at no distant day be dispensed with altogether.

All the lanterns are provided with lightning-rods, with platinum points, made of large copper-wire rope.

Lamps.

It will be necessary to speak of the arrangement of the lamps when an account is given of the principal properties of the combustibles employed.

VI.—COMBUSTIBLES.

The light-houses of France are nearly all illuminated by lamps fed with colza oil. That oil is produced from colza, (*brassica campestris,*) which is cultivated in various parts of our territory, but chiefly in the department of the North and Normandy. The greater part of the lights of the fourth order have been lighted lately with petroleum or the oil of schiste, and the electric light is now being tried in one of our light-houses. Other modes of producing light have been proposed at different times, but they have not yet been practically applied.

FAT OILS.

Experiments have been made at the Central Establishment of Lights upon the different oils which might be employed in light-house illumination, and it seems useful to report here not only what justifies the preference given to the oil of colza, but what appear to be the conditions to be considered in regard to the productions of other countries, or of economy, which may induce to the employment of oil from other productions.

These experiments were made in 1861 and 1862. The oils were furnished by Messieurs. Guillou, Bucquet & Co. They were, each kind, of excellent quality, except the colza oil from India, for which was substituted, as soon as its inferiority was discovered, the oil from the same production which the corporation of the Trinity Board of England uses in its light-houses.

The different oils tested have been burnt successively in small jacket lamps, in single-wick lamps, and in multiple-wick lamps. The trials were numerous, and the results will be found in the following table:

Names of oils.	Where produced.	Duration of the combustion—		Mean intensity for a consumption of 40 grammes and a duration of 8 hours in a lamp—	
		In a watch light.	In a lamp with 1 wick.	With 1 wick of 0.021*m*.	With 2 wicks of 0.039*m*.
French colza	North of France	36 *h*.	29 *h*.	1.04 *b*.	1.14 *b*.
India colza, from the corporation of Trinity House	British India, oil manufactured in England	40	26	0.95	1.06
India colza, (trade)	British India, oil manufactured in England	4	11	0.39	0.83
Arachide, (earth-nut)	Senegal	39	35	1.05	1.04
Olive	Port Maurice	40	23	1.07	0.89
Spermaceti	N. American fisheries.	27	29	1.05	1.01
Cameline	French Flanders	38	20	0.77	0.94
Ravison	Black Sea	28	23	0.82	0.84
Linseed	Brittany	18	14	0.87	.....
Whale	N. American fisheries.	15	18	0.86	1.05
Sesamum	Syria	14	26	0.73	0.85
Cocoanut*	Cochin China	55	41	1.06	1.18

An absolute value should not be given to these figures, for the same kind of oil gives different results, according to its quality and the length of time which has elapsed since it was made. But it is allowed, with this reserve, to deduce from them useful conclusions. It is seen that the different oils are differently classed, according to the quality of them; that which burns longest in a jacket lamp is not that which sustains combustion longest in an Argand lamp; and that which, for the same quantity consumed, gives the greatest intensity from a single-wick lamp does not possess the same merit when used in double-wick lamps in light-houses. Thus, olive oil, which appeared to possess advantages over colza oil when used in the first-named lamps, was inferior when used in those of the second kind.

The influence which the number of wicks showed was more marked in the lamps of the first order than in the others. Two of these lamps were fed, one with colza oil and the other with olive oil. After burning four hours, the first presented a handsome flame, while the second was with difficulty kept burning, and the mean luminous intensities, for 40 grammes of oil consumed, were respectively 1.24 burner and 1.17 burner. These two lamps were left burning for three hours longer, and the flame of the olive-oil lamp fell to that point where there was no longer any comparison, and the snuffing became indispensable. That operation was proceeded with, but only with the olive-oil lamp, and the com-

* The oil, being in a solid state, at the ordinary temperature, was heated to 35° before being introduced into the lamps, and the temperature of the room at 26° when the experiment was made.

parative experiment continued seven consecutive hours. The mean intensity of the colza-oil flame has been found to be 0.71 burner, with 40 grammes of oil consumed in that time, while that of the flame of the olive-oil lamp was only 0.53 burner. The difference would have been much greater if the wicks of the first had been trimmed at the same time those of the second were. This last fact tends to show that the olive oil deteriorates much more than the colza oil in passing through the burner, where it becomes heated.

Cocoanut oil has given excellent results in a lamp of the first-order. After three-hours' burning, the flame was very brilliant, and had an intensity of 1.35 burner with a consumption of 40 grammes; and at the end of eleven hours, when it became necessary to trim the wicks, it had only decreased to 1.23 burner. It only produces a very small thief on the smallest wick. This oil is used for burning in the light-house at Cape St. Jaques, in Cochin China.

Other elements ought to enter into the consideration of oils than those under discussion; those are, the price and the temperature at which they cease to remain in a fluid state.

The following table shows the mean prices at Paris, which, however, are subject to variations far from narrow limits, the density, the co-efficient of expansion, and the temperature at which they congeal and liquify. These last elements have been determined at the laboratory of the School of Bridges and Roads, by Engineer Mangon, with that precision which characterizes all of his experiments:

Names of oils.	Price per 100 kg.*	Weight of cubic centimetre.		Mean coefficient of dilatation from +10° to +100° centgds.	Temperature, approximative.		Remarks.
		At +10° centigrades.	At +100° centigrades.		To congelation.	To liquefaction.	
	fr.	*gr.*	*gr.*		°	°	
French colza	122	0.9174	0.8583	0.000778	+ 3.1	+ 5.1	The figures of the two last columns are anything but precise. The oil passes from the liquid to the solid state through degrees of viscosity which it is impossible to define. The different results show that the oil is at rest or in motion, and in large or small quantities.
India colza	......†	0.9223	0.8634	0.000764	+ 4.0	+ 4.5	
Arachide	130	0.9199	0.8597	0.000784	+ 2.3	+10.5	
Olive	160	0.9186	0.8479	0.000935	+ 4.0	+ 7.5	
Spermaceti	280	0.8844	0.8259	0.000793	+ 5.0	+ 8.0	
Cameline	115	0.9240	0.8650	0.000764	+ 1.0	+ 7.0	
Ravison	115	0.9202	0.8604	0.000778	+ 2.0	+ 6.0	
Linseed	110	0.9254	0.8654	0.000779	+ 2.0	+ 7.0	
Whale	110	0.9261	....	....	— 5.5	+ 7.6	
Sesamum	130	0.9240	0.8636	0.000783	— 3.0	+ 7.0	
Cocoanut	125	0.9343‡	0.8694	0.00098 §	+19.5	+24.0	

In recapitulation, the oils which appear to be the best for illumination, are those of colza, cocoanut, arachide, olive, spermaceti, and whale

* Price at Paris, not comprising custom-house duties.
† This oil is not brought into the trade at Paris.
‡ A 20°.
§ From 20° to 100°.

oil. The order in which they ought to be classed, following the quality in view, may be seen below:

Duration of the combustion in lamp with one wick.	Intensity in a lamp—		Resistance to congelation.	Inferiority of price in France.
	With one wick.	With multiple wicks.		
Cocoanut	Olive	Cocoanut	English colza	Whale
Arachide	Cocoanut	French colza	French colza	Colza
Spermaceti	Spermaceti	English colza	Whale	Cocoanut
French colza	Arachide	Whale	Olive	Arachide
English colza	French colza	Arachide	Spermaceti	Olive
Olive	English colza	Spermaceti	Arachide	Spermaceti
Whale	Whale	Olive	Cocoanut	

Colza oil (French and English) excels greatly all the other oils in two essential respects: that of intensity in multiple-wick lamps, except cocoanut oil, and that of the resistance in passing into the baked state (crusty) by the action of the temperature. It is not far from the best in regard to the duration of combustion and intensity in single-wick lamps, and it is, above all, greatly superior to olive oil for use in multiple-wick lamps. Finally, in regard to price, it is preferable to all the others, except whale oil, which is otherwise inadmissible on account of the short duration of its combustion, and the necessity for frequently trimming the multiple-wick lamps.

It should be stated that the multiple-wick lamps used in experimenting with these different oils were constructed to burn colza oil, and perhaps the other oils would have given better results from lamps whose forms were better adapted for burning them. No trials have yet been made in that direction, for the reason that the colza oil has, in France, an incontestible superiority, and possesses higher claims than all the others; but the engineers of the light-house service design to undertake them in the interest of our colonies in which maritime illumination appears to be beginning to extend and to receive attention.

LAMPS.

In all the lamps fed by colza oil, the wicks are cylindrical, and are placed between two currents of air, so that the combustion may be as active as possible. The glass chimney is contracted at a certain height above the burner, so as to project the air against the middle and upper parts of the flame.

The number of wicks varies with the order of the light, as has been said before.

The following table shows the number and dimensions of the wicks, the consumption of oil, and repeats the figures already given in regard to the flames and their luminous intensities:

Order of light.	No. of wicks.	Mean diameter of wicks in millimetres.*				Dimensions of the flame.		Luminous intensity.	Consumption of oil per hour.	
		No. 1.	No. 2.	No. 3.	No. 4.	Diameter.	Height.		Per burner.	Per luminous unity.
						mm.	*mm.*	*b.*	*gr.*	*gr.*
1st order	4	22	43	64	85	90	100	23.0	760	33.0
2d order	3	24	46	69	....	75	80	15.0	500	33.3
3d order: large model	2	19	39	....	....	45	70	5.0	175	35.0
3d order: small model	2	16	32	....	....	38	65	3.0	110	36.7
4th order: large model	1	24	....	....	....	30	45	1.6	60	37.5
4th order: small model	1	21	....	....	....	27	37	1.3	50	38.5

It is seen that the burners of multiple wicks are preferable to the others, in so far as the economy of light is concerned, since the luminous intensities increase in a greater proportion than the consumption. The figures in the last column exhibit very clearly that merit.

To prevent the burners from becoming too much heated by the action of the flames to which they are exposed, it is necessary to cause much more oil to pass through them than is consumed, and that arrangement is besides favorable to the brilliancy, in maintaining the flame in its normal state. Experience has shown that at least three times as much oil should pass through the burners as is consumed. Thus the lamps are regulated so as to cause to pass through the burner, per hour:

In the first-order lights .... 3.040 *kg.* of oil.
In the second-order lights.................. 2.000 " "
In those of the third order: large model..... 0.700 " "
In those of the third order: small model..... 0.440 " "

Some keepers exceed these figures in a much greater proportion, so as to manage their lights with greater ease; but it may be remarked that that excess of feeding has the effect of raising to a certain extent the most brilliant point of the flame, which, consequently, renders it necessary to modify the distance to be observed between the crown of the burner and the focus of the apparatus.

Plate 15 represents the different kinds of lamp burners, and the flames produced by them. These drawings are made half-size. It was not considered necessary to include the small models of the third and fourth order.

Figure 1 gives the plan of a burner of the first order seen from above, and Figure 2 represents, on one side, the elevation, and on the other, the section taken along the line A B of the plan.

* 1 millimetre = 0.03937 inches.

Figures 3 and 4, 5 and 6, 7 and 8, give, respectively, the plan, elevation, and the section of the burners and the flames of second, third, and of fourth-order constant-level lamps.

These drawings show exactly all that enters into the composition of a lamp burner, but it appears unnecessary to enter here into the details which the instructions upon the light-house service explain fully.

Figures 9 and 10 relate to the oil of schiste, which will be noticed further on.

The most of the lamps having but one-wick burners, and some of those of the third order, smaller model, are of the kind called *constant level*. These lamps are too well known to require to be described. It is known that their reservoir is enclosed in the body of the lamp, and carries at its lower end a valve which opens the moment it is put in place, and causes it to communicate with the burner. Below that valve is a small tube which regulates the height of oil in the burner, whose lower extremity should be held at some millimetres below the crown of the burner. The capillarity causes the oil to rise in the wick.

That arrangement is inadmissible when the flame is required to illuminate the entire horizon, and then recourse is had to lower reservoir lamps in which the ascension of the oil is produced by a mechanism. The only lamps of this description actually used in the light-house service are the *moderator lamps*. Their mechanism is placed in the reservoir, and consists of a spiral spring whose base is fixed in leather, placed upon the oil which forces it up through a tube which traverses it, and comes out below the burner. The movement of the oil is regulated by an iron stem fixed to the burner, which is fitted in the tube upon a length which is reduced in proportion as the piston goes down, and the tension of the spring diminishes. The oil flows to the burner in excess, and that which is not consumed flows back in the reservoir.

With the exception which has been spoken of above, all the lamps of the three largest orders are mechanical lamps.

Those which Messieurs. Fresnel and Arago employed in their experiments of 1821 were the constant-level lamps; the reservoir, more elevated than the burner, received the air through a sliding tube in a leather box, which could be raised or lowered at will, so as to regulate the level of the flow as required. But this system appeared to be ill adapted in practice, on account of the large volume required as well for the reservoir as for the cistern designed to receive the surplus of oil, and, besides, the obligation which it imposed to cause the oil to be replaced in the reservoir from time to time.

The mechanical lamps in most general use in the light-houses are of two kinds:

1st. *Clock-work movement lamp, system of Wagner.*—It has for motor an exterior weight which descends in a column of the armature of the apparatus. An alternating movement of rotation is transmitted to two vertical arbors by means of cranks and wheel-work used in clocks. These arbors traverse the oil reservoir, and are armed by two fixed levers at their upper extremities, which put the feed pumps in play. A fly-wheel regulates the motion of the mechanism. The supply of oil to the burner may be moderated, besides, by turning an endless screw placed in the body of the pumps, and arranged so as to reduce in proportion to the accession the opening designed to introduce the combustible.

2d. *Moderator lamp, by weights.*—A cast-iron piston, fitted with leather stamped on its circumference, is weighted, and moves with little friction in the body of the lamp. A chain wound around a horizontal arbor allows it to be wound up. It descends by the action of the weights, and causes the movement which raises the oil in a vertical tube. The regulator consists of an orifice of small diameter, occupying the upper part of this tube, in which a conical needle passes, and raised more or less, according as it becomes necessary to increase or diminish the flow. In some of these lamps the movement of the needle is regulated by that of the piston, so that the orifice, opening in a measure as the piston descends, overcomes a greater pressure.

The instructions for the light-house service furnish minute details in regard to the composition and the attendance upon the lamps, and render unnecessary further development here of this subject.

WICKS.

The quality of the wicks exerts a marked influence upon the regularity of the flame, and above all upon its being properly maintained. It is essential that they should be woven of cotton of excellent quality; that their tissue be uniform; also as supple as possible, and neither too openly nor too closely woven. Specimen samples, adopted after a long course of experiments, have been deposited at the central Light-house Establishment in Paris, and all new wicks are required to conform strictly to them. The woof is of cotton, in wicks which should offer a certain degree of resistance, and such are required for sideral apparatus, which are not as well kept up as the others; it is of silk for the most of the lamps.

The table below shows the sizes (width) of the wicks when laid flat, the number of ends of each strand, the kind of woof, and the weight per metre of length.

Order of lights and number of wicks.			Width, in millimetres.*	Number of ends.	Nature of the woof.	Weight per meter, in grammes.†
1st order	wick No. 1		34	8	Silk	35
	wick No. 2		65	8	Silk	67
	wick No. 3		97	9	Silk	107
	wick No. 4		132	9	Silk	145
2d order	wick No. 1		36	8	Silk	37
	wick No. 2		71	8	Silk	73
	wick No. 3		106	9	Silk	118
3d order	large pattern	wick No. 1	30	8	Silk	30
		wick No. 2	61	9	Silk	65
	small pattern	wick No. 1	24	8	Silk	22
		wick No. 2	48	9	Silk	53
4th order	large burner		38	10	Cotton	42
	small burner		33	9	Silk	36
Siderals	large burner		38	10	Cotton	41
	small burner		29	10	Cotton	32
"Photophore," carcel burner			30	8	Silk	32

The wicks of lamps for petroleum or oil of schiste have cotton woof.

It is of great importance that the wicks be kept free from dust and the effects of dampness, to place them regularly in the burners, and to trim them with the greatest care and precision.

GLASS CHIMNEYS AND DAMPERS.

The burners of all lamps are covered by glass chimneys formed with long curved elbows. Above each of these is enclosed, without being fastened laterally, a regulator or damper made of sheet iron, which is used to regulate the combustion in conjunction with it. In the lens apparatus of the fourth order, the regulator or damper is supported upon the upper crown of the armature; in the others, it is kept at its summit by a sheet-iron sheath which is fixed to the apparatus. That sheath is always open at its upper end, and the products of the combustion are freely raised to escape outside, in passing first through the openings of the chimney of the cupola, and afterwards by those of the bowl which covers them, as shown by Figure 1 of Plate 9. In some light-houses the sheath has been closed at the top and three sheet-iron tubes, fixed upon its cover, have been arranged for conducting the products of the combustion into the chimney of the cupola, so as to preserve all the parts of the lantern free from smoke. This system is shown by the Figures 1 of Plates 6, 7, and 8.

The chimney of the lamp is supported by a cylindrical holder, which is raised or lowered by turning it to the left or to the right. Too high, the chimney renders the flame reddish with diminished brilliancy; too

*1 millimetre = 0.03937 inch.

†1 gramme = 15.444 grains, Troy. 1 gramme = 0.035 ounce, avoirdupois.

low, it increases the brilliancy, and diminishes the height of the flame. The same effects may be produced by the proper movement of the key of the damper; the flame lowers and whitens in proportion as the passage is opened; it rises, reddens, and tends to become smoky, when the opening is reduced in size.

MINERAL, PETROLEUM, OR SCHISTE OIL.

The oils which have been used advantageously within a few years past, both for domestic purposes and for lighting many of our small light-houses and beacons, are not included among those already spoken of, for the reason, that they differ entirely from all others in every respect, and cannot be burnt in the same kind of lamps; these are the essential oils of schiste and petroleum.

The first of these oils is produced from distillation of bituminous schiste; the second is produced principally in North America, where large quantities have been recently found. These are from the hydrocarbons.

The densities of those which are best adapted to illumination vary from 0.80 to 0.83, taking the density of water for unity. When more dense, they are difficult to burn, and tend greatly to create a thick smoke; when lighter, they are liable to cause serious accidents, inasmuch as they become too inflammable.

These oils possess, compared to the fatty oils, the triple merit of being less expensive, produce more light for the same amount of consumption, and give lower flames, and less useless divergence in the small apparatus; but they are more apt to smoke in case the current of air is not properly regulated, and the attendance upon them requires much more care than with the others.

From the numerous experiments to which these oils have been subjected, the following results have been reported:

1. The oil of schiste or petroleum, of suitable quality, gives about one burner of carcel for 30 grammes consumed per hour.

2. The lamps used in the light-house service, which have a burner of 0.0255*m.* of diameter, burn about 70 grammes per hour during the first hours of lighting, and only 52 grammes at the end of twelve or fifteen hours; for a lamp well attended, a mean consumption of 65 grammes per hour may be allowed, and an intensity of 2.2 burners.

3. Petroleum and the oil of schiste act about alike.

In estimating the price of colza oil at 1.51 franc per kilogramme, and that of petroleum or schiste at 1.10 franc, delivered at the light-stations, it is seen that the unity of light comes to $1.51\,fr. \times 0.040 = 0.06\,fr.$ with colza oil, and to $\frac{1.10\,fr. \times 0.065}{2.2} = 0.033\,fr.$ with the others, deduction being made for the cost of wicks, chimneys, &c.

Two descriptions of lamps are used for these new oils; one is the ordinary constant-level lamp, regulated so that the level of the oil maintains itself at about 0.04*m.* below the crown of the burner; the other consists of a simple reservoir in which the wick is thrust, and from which the oil rises by capillarity in sufficient quantity, so long as the level does not descend 0.16*m.* below the burner.

The first consume a little more, and are in a manner more self-sustaining than the second, and they give consequently a better flame, which continues more uniform during the entire combustion; but they do not offer other facilities for the service, and they are not adapted to lights required to illuminate the entire horizon.

The burner of these lamps has a double current of air, but that is not sufficient to insure complete combustion—above all, a long combustion—and it is necessary to fit upon it a small brass disk, which throws the air upon the interior face of the flame and cools the wick. This arrangement is represented by the Figures 9 and 10 of Plate 15. Figure 9 is in plan taken from above, and Figure 10 gives, on one side, the elevation, and on the other, a section through A B of the burner and the reservoir. The screw for moving the wick is seen upon that section.

The chimneys are enlarged at the bottom so as to unite the form of the flame.

That form necessitates a special profile for lens apparatus illuminated with petroleum or oil of schiste, or at least a modification of the positions of the catadioptric rings, as has been seen in discussing the question of illuminating apparatus.

Some schiste or petroleum lamps are supplied with flat wicks, which are thrust into a lower reservoir. They have not the brass disk, and the forms of the chimneys are not special.

All the efforts thus far made, to apply the oil of schiste to the illumination of the three largest orders of lights, have been unsuccessful. They did not succeed in giving much more intensity to the flame without causing it to smoke and rendering it very difficult to manage. Some success has been obtained by insufflation of air; but the system has not appeared to be susceptible of practical application, and the result left, besides, much yet to be desired.

GASEOUS COMBUSTIBLES.

Other modes of producing light have been proposed at different times; but they have not been thought worthy of being adopted for light-house illumination, and it will be sufficient to mention them in making known very succinctly the reasons for rejecting them.

Hydrogen gas produced by the distillation of bituminous coal is more economical than colza oil, about in the same proportion as the oil of schiste. It brings the price of the unity of light per hour to about 0.03 *fr.* The objections to it are, that it does not give a flame as brilliant on the surface equal to that of oil, and the danger of causing explosions. The gas from oil produces a very beautiful flame, but it has not the merit of economy, and does not offer more security than the other.

Oxygen gas, employed to vivify any flame whatever, has produced excellent results as regards the luminous intensity. The cost of this gas and the fear of explosions have caused it to be rejected.

The oxyhydrogen or Drummond light has been recommended many times, and has received modifications more or less beneficial. The expense of it, the danger which attends it, and the irregularity of its movements, have not allowed its practical use in light-houses. Its luminous intensity is not, besides, very great; it varied from three to six burners in the tests to which it has been subjected.

ELECTRIC LIGHT.

For a long time the electric light from currents produced by batteries of different descriptions, especially from that of Bunsen, has been asked for. The results obtained have been excellent so far as the luminous intensity is concerned, but the manipulations necessary for the apparatus, the chances of extinction, the irregularity of the products, and the greatly-increased expense, do not seem to warrant the application of this mode of producing light for the illumination of light-houses.

A new arrangement, based upon the induction currents developed by the magnets, has made a long step on this subject, and, after having been experimented with for three years at the central Light-house Establishment at Paris, it is now applied upon trial at one of the first-order fixed lights at Cape La Hève, near Havre.

Mechanism.

The magneto-electric machine which produces currents* is represented in section by the Figure 25, below. It is composed of forty horse-shoe magnets, distributed by five equidistant vertical planes, upon the edges of a right-angle prism with an octagonal base, and the bobbins passing between the groups of magnets closely placed. These bobbins are fixed upon the circumference of vertical disks, which revolve around the axis of the prism, and are put in motion by a small steam engine. The bobbins number thirty-two. There are eight to the disk, as well as there are eight magnets in each vertical plane. The poles of the magnets alternate upon each of the horizontal ranges in

* This machine belongs to the Alliance Company, which has patented it.

such a way that one bobbin is always placed between two opposite poles, and but one current establishes itself in the wire which surrounds it, from which it approaches one magnet, afterwards reverses from the one from which it goes. Sixteen changes of direction correspond to each revolution of the cylinder. The maximum of intensity was obtained when the machine made from 350 to 400 turns per minute, and the current then changes nearly one hundred times per second. The partial currents of the same kind reunite, and are alternately put in communication with the one and the other of the cheeks of the frame of cast iron of the machine, which are separated by insulating substances. It is at the summit of these cheeks where the conducting wires are fixed which take, successively, the total currents to conduct them to the electric lamp. These wires are covered by an insulating material throughout their entire length.

FIG. 25.

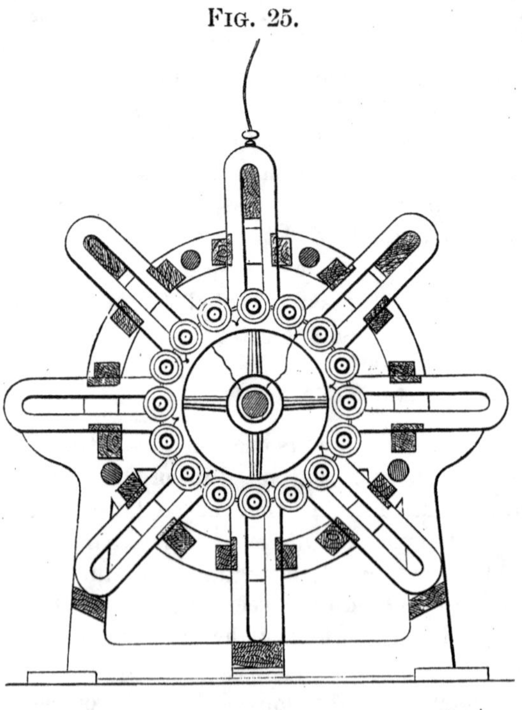

The magnets have each the power of 60 kilogrammes.

The steam engine is of high pressure, and of nearly four-horse power, when the tension of the steam in the boiler is carried to six atmospheres, and it suffices for four atmospheres and a half to give the normal velocity to two machines similar to that described. It is fed by fresh water, which is collected and retained in large cisterns.

Regulator.

The carbon points, which produce the light, are supported and maintained at a proper distance by a regulator or electric lamp. That apparatus has for its object to bring the two points near to each other, so that they will burn without coming in contact, which would cause their extinction. Numerous systems of great ingenuity have been conceived for that purpose. All of them are based upon the same principle—upon the intervention of an electro-magnet which traverses the currents.

That which has been adopted for the illuminating apparatus of the light-house at La Hève is by Mr. Serrin. It consists of the following:

Two carbon carriers are fitted each to a vertical stem, which moves in one sheath. These stems are so bound together that when the lower one rises the other descends, so that the last is moved by its weights. This movement is moderated and regulated by a fly with toothed wheels. The sheath of the lower pencil carrier is supported by a double parallelogram, jointed, which is fitted with a small stop stem, which, according as it descends or rises, unites with one of the wheels and stops the movement, or leaves it free and allows the carbon points to come near to each other. This parallelogram is subjected to two opposite forces; one produced by a spiral spring tends to raise it, the other, due to two electro-magnets which traverse the current, tends to lower it, in drawing a fixed armature to the lower part of that piece.

The apparatus is regulated in such a manner that, when the carbon points are at the desired distance for the production of the light, the wheel-work is united, which insures the immobility of the carbon holders. That distance increases with the combustion, the current becomes weakened, the electro-magnet loses its power, the parallelogram yields to the spring and raises the uniting stem, the carbon carriers are immediately put in motion, approach each other, and do not stop until the moment is reached when the current has regained sufficient intensity to determine a new connection.

The current which passes through the electro-magnets is that which unites the lower carbon point.

Although the currents pass alternately from one to the other carbon point, experience has shown that the lower one is consumed a little faster than the other, at a rate which varies, as the matter is not perfectly homogeneous, and which appears to be about $\frac{108}{100}$. Consequently the diameters of the pulleys, upon which the chains used to unite the movements of the two stems, are regulated so that the position of the luminous focus does not change, or at least does not vary beyond very restricted limits. That effect has only recently been verified, and it was not estimated at first at its true value.

The consumption of the carbon points will have the effect of altering the existing relation between the weights of the two stems, and consequently the movement of the system. That inconvenience has been remedied by means of a small chain wound at one of its extremities around the lower stem, and the other upon a fixed point; the stem supports a longer part as the carbons become shorter.

Other dispositions of detail ought to be mentioned:

1. A button moving up the arm of a lever, which carries two pullies to bring back the chain of the two stems, allows the luminous focus to

be raised or lowered within practical limits, without interrupting the movement of the mechanism.

2. Another button moves upon the spiral spring in such a way that the machine may be easily regulated to suit the intensity of the current. It is evident that the spring ought to be much tighter, as the current, which is antagonistic to it, is more powerful.

3. The stops properly placed at different parts of the system limit the extent of the movement.

4. A kind of small crutch, turning around the summit of the upper sheath, allows the carbons to be placed very regularly in the position and at the desired distance, and the upper carbon may be brought exactly in the axis of the other by means of buttons which regulate the movements of their carriers in every direction horizontally.

5. The carbon carriers are liable to be burnt, if after the consumption of the carbons they come too near to each other, and the machine is so fixed that they are still distant 0.06*m*. when they have reached the limit of their course.

6. A box of brass covers the whole of the machinery, and protects it from dust and moisture.

This machinery is sufficiently complicated, without always being so much so as to make it necessary to have the pieces before one's eyes to describe it without difficulty; but it is solidly placed; each of its parts offers more resistance than is rigorously necessary, and it appears to be of a kind which presents neither difficulty in attending upon it, nor requiring frequent repairs. It satisfies all the special conditions demanded of it in practice.*

Carbons.

The coal points have a square section of 0.007*m*. of the side; they are 0.27*m*. long, which gives to each 0.20*m*. for burning, the remainder being lost on account of the carriers covering a part, and, besides, not coming in contact.

Their quality has a great influence upon the length of time they burn, and at the same time upon the intensity of the light. Those which are now employed are made of the densest of the deposits of the

* A new regulator is now being tried by the light-house-service engineers, and everything leads to the hope that it will give better results. Conceived by Mr. Faucault, (to whom electric illumination owes already a most ingenious automatic apparatus and the substitution of angular carbons in place of those hitherto employed,) it has been constructed most perfectly by one of our most skilled artists, Mr. Duboscq. The mechanism consists of a differential movement joining to two wheels which may be geared either simultaneously or alternating, by the pallet of the bent lever which causes the regulating bobbin to move so as to cause the arrest, approach, or recoil of the carbons automatically. The apparatus is extremely sensitive.

carbon which form in the retorts for distilling coal. Their mean consumption may be estimated at 0.05*m.* per hour, exclusive of the waste.

Luminous intensity.

The intensity of the light generated by the apparatus about to be described, presents great variations, caused not by the electric current, (that is constant so long as the motion is the same,) but for want of homogeneousness of the coal points, the slight modifications in the form and the distance between the points, and, above all, by the displacement of the voltaic arc, which moves from one side to the other. It is very difficult to measure it by the photometer, for the reason that these variations are incessant; however, it has been done when it was known a sufficient degree of precision could be had. In the actual state of things, that intensity may be estimated at the mean value of 125 burners, a maximum value of 180 burners, and a minimum of about 75 burners. Placed in an apparatus for a fixed light like that at La Hève, which is represented on page 76, (Figure 22,) this luminous focus gives a divergence of about 6° in the vertical plane, and a mean intensity in the flame most illuminated which ought to be valued at 3,500 burners, deducting the rays absorbed by the plate-glass of the lantern.

The electric light has not yet been applied to eclipse-light apparatus, but there is no serious difficulty in making the application. The intensity of the flashes will vary with the angular space which the lenses may embrace, and might reach to about 30,000 burners.

Electric light at La Hève.

The uninterrupted exhibition of lights, which is of primary importance in light-houses, requires the adoption of proper measures to anticipate any extinctions to which they may be liable, whether on account of the necessity for renewing the carbons, or of accidents to the machinery or the electric lamp. It has been deemed prudent to have in the same establishment a double set of all the parts of the system. In that way there is, besides, the additional advantage of being able, if desired, in the time of fog, for example, to put the two magneto-electric machines in motion, and thereby double the brilliancy of the light.

The dispositions adopted for the light-houses at La Hève, which illuminate three-fourths of the horizon, are as follows:

Two steam engines and two electric machines have been placed, as shown by Figure 26, in a temporary building on the west front of the south tower.

A A, steam engines; B B, magneto-electric machines; C, water tank and depot for carbons below; D, the tower; E E, India-rubber tube into the lantern; F F, conducting wires.

The two electrical machines may be put in motion separately, or both together, in such a way as to be conducted by a single motor. A very simple mechanism allows, for that purpose, to unite the two axes or to render them independent of each other.

The conducting wires ought to pass up through the interior of the tower, but in the execution of the works they have been placed in a vertical case outside, against one of the reëntering angles of the structure. They are kept in their position by porcelain insulators.

FIG. 26.

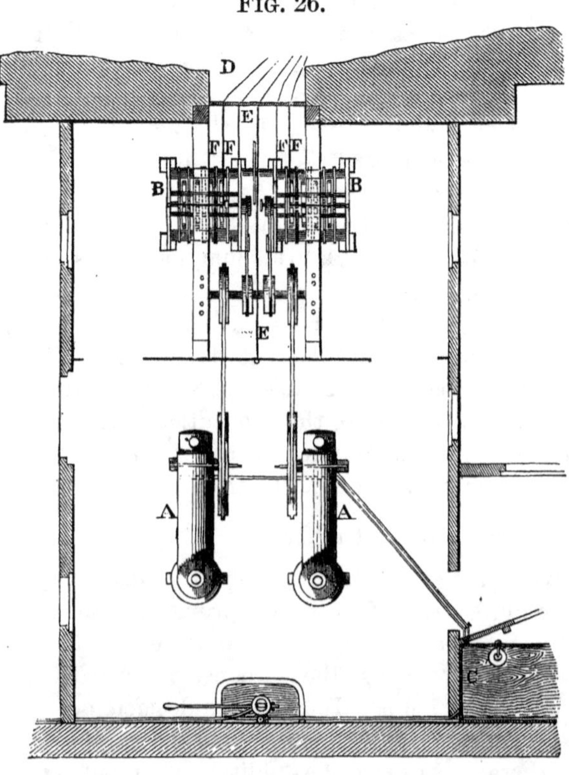

The catadioptric apparatus are placed in the same lantern which has been established in front upon one of the angles of a square chamber, divided into two stories, which takes the place above the platform of the tower, the old lantern and its base, (see Plate 19,) and has been put outside, in harmony with the rest of the idifice. The plan (Figure 27) shows that arrangement.

A, first room; B, stairway of the tower; C, steps leading to the upper chamber; D, door to the outside platform; K K, iron roads for the regulators; L, the lantern; O, illuminating apparatus; R, spare regulator; S, luminous rays emanating from the small lens; T T, conducting wires; U, commutator; V, India-rubber tube. The amplitude and the position of the sea horizon are represented by the arc of the circle *m n p*.

The lantern rests on its base upon a massive masonry, and it is sustained laterally by two uprights of cast iron secured at the bottom, united at their summit by a lintel of the same material, and fixed upon the walls upon which they rest. The plate-glass of the lantern is curved and kept in place above and below by bronze sashes, without being laterally by the vertical uprights, which will determine the occultations with regard to the diameter of the flame. This glazing is composed of two parts, each placed to the right of one of the lens apparatus, and having not more than 0.55*m.* of height. The dome of the lantern is formed outside by bands of sheet iron which give rigidity to the system.

FIG. 27.

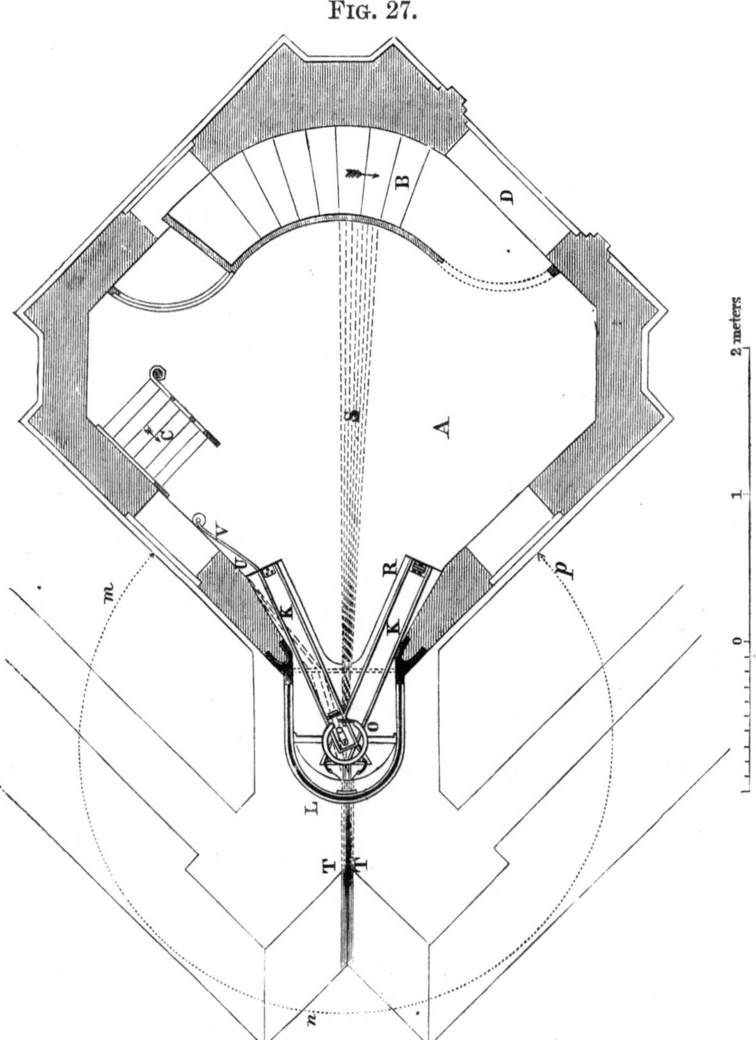

The vertical section, which is taken through the axis of the apparatus (Figure 28) shows the dispositions which have been made.

A A, the illuminating apparatus; B B, railroads for the lamps or regulators; C C, conducting wires; D D, commutators; E E, India-rubber tube.

The apparatus are open for one-fourth of the circle, and may be turned around to facilitate in cleaning them.

FIG. 28.

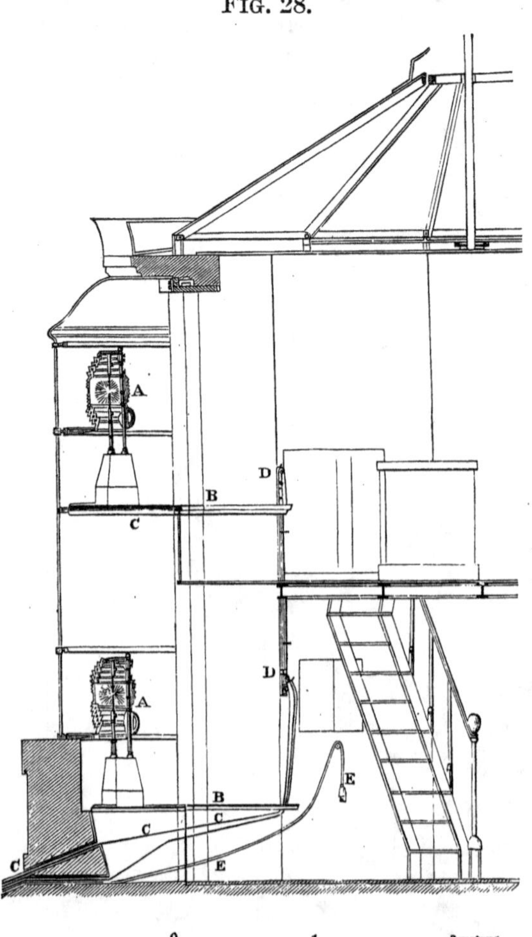

Two electric lamps are assigned to each apparatus; they enter and slide upon the small railroads which cross and support a cast-iron service table; they stop when they reach the desired point, then taking the currents and instantly lighting. For that purpose, the iron table is in communication with one of the conducting wires, and the other wire in contact with an electric comb *(peigne electrique)* which is fixed upon that table, below the lens apparatus, with the interposition of an insulating substance, and presses with its elastic teeth a metallic plate placed under the lamp. That plate conducts in the electro-magnets the current which it receives. The other current is introduced into the body of the lamp, in passing by the railroad. The time necessary for the substitution of one lamp for another does not exceed two seconds.

The existence of a duplicate apparatus, always ready for use, allows means, besides, of preventing, for however short a time, the extinction which that operation causes. Whenever the lighted lamp ought to be removed, for any cause whatever, and always for renewing the carbons, a commutator placed under the control of the keeper, allows the instantaneous passing of the current into the other apparatus, and the intensity of the light is diminished for only a very short time. All the operations are executed with the greatest facility.

It is very important, in view of the restricted dimensions of the light and of the illuminating apparatus, that the position of the luminous focus should vary only within very narrow limits; a displacement of 0.005*m.*, in any direction, would cause an elevation or depression of about 2° of the beam of light emanating from the apparatus, and no ray will be carried to the limit of the horizon, if the error reaches to 0.008*m.* But, in admitting that the keepers will fully appreciate the necessity for keeping the variations within the limits of some millimetres, it would be hard to impose upon them the obligation to have their eyes continually upon a light of such great intensity, that the colored glasses of green or blue will not relieve them unless of so deep a color as to be seen through an ordinary light. The service has been facilitated, and one of the gravest inconveniences attendant upon electric illumination partly remedied, by means of a small lens which, placed in the dead angle of the apparatus, throws against the opposite side of the chamber an amplified and renewed image of the light, (S, Figure 27.) The amplification is such, that an actual variation of 0.001*m.* corresponds to a represented variation of 0.022*m.* The keeper is not required, nor is it necessary for him, to look at the electric light, but at the image, to satisfy himself of the continuation of the proper operation of the apparatus, and the least deviation shows itself with the greatest preciseness.

The study of the means of regularly registering the extinctions and the displacements of the focus, without the intervention of the keeper, upon a paper sensible to the action of the light, has been commenced, and is still prosecuted.

COMPARATIVE MERIT OF THE ELICTRIC LIGHT.

To estimate the merit of the electric light, in so far as relates to the economy of expense, the comparison should not be limited, as has been done for the oil of schiste, to establish the cost of the combustible consumed. This light necessitates the employment of expensive material, as well as the attendance upon a machine besides the lamp, and these two sources of expense cannot be omitted.

The calculation would seem to be as follows:

Cost of the first establishing:

Magneto-electric machine of four disks	8000. 00 *fr.*
Steam engine and accessories	3000. 00
Regulator, conducting wires, &c	1500. 00
Total	12500. 00

In calculating at ten per cent. interest, and the extinguishment of that sum, admitting, as in our lights, 4,000 hours of combustion annually, and allowing two furnaces to the steam engine, the expense per hour will be found from the following figures:

Interest and funding of the capital, 1,250 *fr.*, will be per hour	0. 3125 *fr.*
Fuel for the steam engine, 10 *kg.* at 40 *fr.*, the 1,000 *kg.*	0. 4000
Salaries of two firemen, 2,800 *fr.* per annum, and per hour	0. 7000
Salaries of two keepers, 2,000 *fr.* per annum, and per hour	0. 5000
Carbon, 0.16*m.* per hour, including waste, at 2.25 *fr.* the metre	0. 3600
Lubricating oil, water, attendance, &c	0. 1275
Expense per hour	2. 4000

The mean luminous intensity being estimated at 125 burners, the cost of one burner per hour, for the light burning freely in space, comes to 0.0192 *fr.*

The cost of the same quantity of light, when it is furnished by a first-order lamp fed by colza oil, may be estimated as follows:

Interest and funding the cost of the lamp, ten per cent. per annum, will be 65 *fr.* and per hour	0. 0163 *fr.*
Salaries of two keepers as above	0. 5000
760 *gr.* of oil per hour, at 1. 51 *fr*	1. 1476
Wicks and glass chimneys, 119 *fr.* per annum, and per hour	0. 0298
Attendance, waste, &c	0. 0583
Expense per hour	1. 7520

The luminous intensity being equal to 23 burners, the cost per hour and per burner is 0. 0762 *fr.*

If the cost of the unity of light obtained with colza oil, burnt in a lamp of the first order, be represented by 1, the electric machine will give the same quantity of light for 0.252 *fr.*

The second of these modes of production is near to four times more economical than the other, under the conditions which have served as a basis of our calculations. If the source of the electric light were of less intensity, the cost of the luminous unity would be increased, for the principal elements which constitute it are independent, within a certain limit, of the quantity of light produced. And, on the other hand, if the currents are made more intense in their development, the cost per hour is increased, but will reduce the cost of the unity of light. One of the inconveniences of the electric light, in its present state of development, is that it is not adapted economically to lights of feeble intensities.

To estimate justly the advantages which this light presents for light-house illumination, it will be necessary to include in the account the cost of the lens apparatus and of duplicate machinery, as well as the cost of construction necessary to the establishment and placing of the machinery and the furnaces and boilers, and to take into account the interest to navigation to have the intensity of the light increased. It is not deemed necessary to enter into a discussion upon this subject, since the conclusions must vary according to the circumstances which are presented, and the figures, as well as the methods of calculation shown in this memoir, furnish all the other elements of questions of this sort, which may be called in for treatment.

There is, nevertheless, a reserve in presenting this subject; it ought to be observed, however, that of the lights of different kinds to which the photometer assigns the same intensity have not always the same range. It has been seen, when the question of colored lights was under review, that the red rays increased more freely in the atmosphere than the white ones, while the green ones appeared to be in the reverse way, so that the range depends at the time upon the intensity and the nature of the light. A luminous focus may be very brilliant, and at the same time have but a very limited range during the existence of certain kinds of fog, if the red rays cause its defect. An experiment made by the engineers of the light-house service upon a new mode of producing the electric light conceived in England, comes in to the support of that assertion. A thin fillet of mercury falling into a capsule was substituted for the coal points; the light had an intensity analogous to that obtained with them, and two apparatus, the one of mercury and the other of carbons (coal points) lighted simultaneously, appeared equal at the distance of 1,500 metres in a calm atmosphere. But red, colored glasses having been placed before them, the first was almost completely extinguished, while the other retained a very handsome brilliancy. The green color produced an entirely different result, as was expected; the light by coal points (carbons) is not extinct, but it is not much more brilliant than the other. It was concluded from these experiments, that if useful, as it might be under many aspects, the system which was employed was probably not of a nature to be applied to the illumination of light-houses, and the inventor has not kept the promise which he made, to submit his system to new trials.

But observations made upon the electric light actually in use, both at long and short distances, tend to establish the conclusion that, as at present composed, it is inferior to the light produced by colza oil. These experiments are still in progress, as the observations made are not sufficiently numerous to warrant the enunciation of formal conclusions.

CHAPTER III (LIGHT-HOUSE STRUCTURES) has been omitted in the translation.

CHAPTER IV (LIST OF FRENCH LIGHTS to January 1, 1864) has also been omitted.

PART II.

CHAPTER I (Beacons, Buoys, and Light-vessels) has been omitted.

CHAPTER II.—Harbor Tide-Signals has been omitted.

II.—FOG-SIGNALS.

The proper signals to be made during fogs and thick weather, to indicate to navigators the entrance to a port, or the position of a danger, have been objects of numerous studies; but the question which they raise has not yet been regarded as solved.

The entrances to the greater part of our ports are marked in foggy and thick weather by bells which are sounded at will, with suitable variations of intervals, and some of the isolated light-stations on the sea-coast are also provided with similar apparatus; in the United States of America, where fogs seem to be more frequent than they are on our sea-coast, they have not hesitated, on account of the great expense, to provide sound as an aid to navigation, but have established at a great many points, fog-bells weighing 1,000 lbs. and over, sounded by clock-work machinery, and at other places powerful whistles worked by compressed air.*

Numerous experiments were made in 1854 by the Lighting Service Engineers upon different instruments, which seemed to be of a character from which good results might be expected.

DIFFERENT INSTRUMENTS.

Fire-arms having been discarded on account of the inconvenience and danger attending their use, or at least the supplies they require for use, the apparatus successively tried were bells, tam-tams, and a kind of large rattle made of wood, such as is used in the East, metallic plates, trumpets, and whistles. The clock-work-movement bells, whistles, and trumpets were at once found to be superior to all the others. And at the same time, among these last, there are some of them which, at a short distance, produce a very lively impression upon the ear. We will cite especially the tam-tams, which are used in England on board

---

* Since the date of this Memoir, (November, 1864,) the U. S. Light-house Board has made a great many experiments with sounding instruments, with the view to the adoption of the one best suited to give warning during fogs, snow storms, and thick weather.

Steam whistles, trumpets, sirens, and bells, are in use at present. T. A. J.

of most of the light-vessels. They cannot be heard much over 500 metres, but they possess the merit of emitting a characteristic sound, which recommends it. A trumpet made by Mr. Darche, a capable manufacturer of musical instruments, has been heard at a much greater distance than either one of the other instruments. It is terminated by a mouth in the form of a paraboloid of revolution, and is provided with a reed valve, which a spiral spring maintains opposite to the opening by which the air comes, and which vibrates under the double action of this spring and the elastic force of the gas. Its sounds have been heard at more than two kilometres'* distance, against a strong wind, while a bell of 100 kilogrammes could not be heard more than 700 metres.

But the range of that instrument diminishes in proportion as the observer is removed from its direction, and if it be necessary to make it heard upon a horizon of a prescribed amplitude, it will be necessary to give to it a rotating motion during calm weather, so as to give the greatest intensity of sound successively on all the lines of direction.

The whistles, similar to those used on locomotives, cannot be heard so far as the trumpets of which we have spoken, but they possess the advantage of distributing uniformly around the horizon, and if no great importance is to be attached to that merit, it is probable that, by means of a reflector, properly fitted, their range might be increased so as to give as much, if not more, power to them than the trumpet. May not the sounds produced by them be mistaken for those made by the winds passing through the riggings of the vessels? Would the trumpets be considered more characteristic? These questions cannot be sufficiently answered except by numerous experiments made at sea. Besides, these instruments present the grave inconvenienc of requiring to be compressed to several atmospheres, and to expend a like quantity when it becomes necessary to make them heard at sufficiently short intervals of time, rendering it necessary to have recourse to machinery to keep up the amount of consumption.

It has not been judged, in the actual state of things, that the navigation of our coast has sufficient interest to require sounds to be heard at a great distance to justify the expense which the establishment and maintenance of these machines would entail.

BELLS.

The bells then remain. They involve the following questions:

At what distance can they be heard, according to their calibre and the force and direction of the wind?

What dispositions are required to be made to increase their range?

What are the modes of striking the best adapted to render the sig-

* 2,187 yards.

nals characteristic, and prevent their confusion with sounds produced by other bells?

What is the mode of placing applicable under most circumstances?

In regard to ranges, observations have been made in the ports of Cherbourg and Boulogne. They have established that the noise which may be made by the stroke of a hammer upon a bell is heard at a greater distance than the sounds of several bells together, and still greater as the strokes, each one being distinct, are more rapid. Thus, the range is increased in the ratio of 1 to 1.14, when the number which was 15 per minute was increased to 25. We admit that we may, with risking the rupture of the bell, make the weight of the hammer falling 0.20*m.* upon a bell of 100 kilogrammes, 5 kilogrammes; and for a bell of 200 kilogrammes, the hammer falling from the same height, may be 9 kilogrammes.

From numerous experiments, it has been concluded that a bell of 100 kilogrammes, well placed, and thus worked, may be heard, during what sailors call a good breeze, at about 1,200 metres distance when the wind is against the sound, at 2,000 metres when it is at right angles to it, and at 4,000 metres when with the wind. During calm weather, or with a light crossing breeze, the range of a bell of this description should be heard at the distance of 2,500 metres. No experiments have been made during violent winds, but we know that, when they blow against them, the strongest and loudest sounds are arrested. We know, also, that, in general, fogs do not exist under such atmospheric circumstances; they almost always come from sea, it is true, but are accompanied by a slight breeze.

The ranges increase with the weight of the bell, and, to a certain point, with the height of the tone. In order to have the sounds, which ought to be heard in succession, distinctly and readily noted, they should have an interval of at least one second of time. The intervals to mark the termination of a number of continuous strokes should not be less than six seconds.

Two means present themselves for increasing the range of a sounding instrument: to have recourse to apparatus of a kind to increase the sound, or to transmit, by way of reflection, the undulations which are otherwise lost in the direction in which they are not required to be heard.

The first has been tried without producing the effects which were desired, at least without sufficiently great benefit to justify the expense. Neither a reinforcing tube nor a large wooden deflector, arranged somewhat like a sideral apparatus, so as to act both by vibration and reflection, have produced sufficiently marked results, and we ceased to continue experiments which were long and expensive. It is probable that greater skill might succeed better. We have abandoned the system without condemning it.

Simple reflection has given increase of range much more marked. Sound was treated as light. A bell was placed in the focus of a large parabolic reflector, or rather a hemispherical one, as a certain amount of divergence was feared, made of material little liable to vibrations. That apparatus, of 1.50*m.* of opening, was formed of an iron shell enveloped in a bed of Portland cement of from 0.06*m.* to 0.08*m.* thickness. The hammers of the bell were put in motion by machinery. The experiments were made in 1861 and 1862, in the harbor of Boulogne, by the engineers, Messrs. Legros and Saint-Ange Allard. The bell with the reflector was placed on the extremity of the west pier, and, for the purpose of comparison, an exactly similar bell was placed immediately above. Each one weighed 100 kilogrammes, producing sensibly the same sound or tone, and were struck by hammers weighing 2.50 kilogrammes at first, and afterwards 5 kilogrammes, which fell from a height of 0.20*m.*, and were immediately after striking released from contact by the springs. The two bells were put in motion in succession, and observers placed upon different points of the sea horizon, embracing a semicircle, made known by signals the moment the sounds were not heard by them. Two observers, suitably stationed on the coast, fixed the exact positions at the time. These points were afterwards noted on a drawing, and they were sufficiently numerous to allow the curve of ranges to be traced of each experiment, with every degree of accuracy which the subject admitted of; then were noted on the curve the ranges of 9° to 9° on each side of the axis of the reflector, which afforded the means of making, in figures, a comparative resumé of the observations.

The experiments were made under different circumstances of intensity and direction of the winds.

If the experiments had been made during a perfect calm, the curve of the ranges of the bell without the reflector would have been an arc of the circle, with the exception of the modifications caused by the position of the hammer, and the other would have been more or less lengthened in the direction of the axis of the reflector and contracted on the sides. But the wind had the effect of altering these curves the most when it was strongest, and it gave to the maximum intensity of the reflector bell nearly the same direction as that of the other bell. The reflector always increased the range in the offing, but not in the lengthening of its axis. The reflected sonorous undulations were carried away very nearly like the others, so that, except during calms, there was no real advantage, contrary to what many persons expected by giving to the reflector a rotary motion in the horizontal plane; but by moving it thus, to all the points of the horizon in succession, the greatest range was not attained.

The summary of the experiments, seven in number, and sufficiently complete to allow of the tracing of the curves referred to, with all the desired exactness, established the mean ratio of the range of the bell without the reflector to that of the one with the reflector to be 100 to 147, in the angular space of 60°, where the sound was heard furthest, and that the bell without the reflector was only superior outside of 100° of the line of the greatest range. It was also found that during calms, or when the wind blew from the bell with the reflector, that the comparative value was increased; the mean ratio of the greatest ranges was found to be about 10 to 17 under these two conditions, while the latter was reduced to 13 under a good breeze which was nearly directly against the direction of the sound.

These results having been obtained, it became necessary to inquire, whether or not an increase of the weights of the bells would give, at less cost, equivalent results to those of the reflector, and a new series of experiments was made, in which two bells were compared, one of 100 kilogrammes with a reflector, the other of 225 kilogrammes without one. The hammers of each fell from a height of 0.20*m.*, and struck sixty times per minute; that of the first weighed 5 kilogrammes, and that of the second 9 kilogrammes. The greatest range of the heaviest bell reached to 6,140 metres, and that of the other to 7,625 metres, with a strong breeze blowing nearly directly from the bell and in the axis of the reflector. In an angular space of 60°, comprising the arc of greatest ranges, the mean ratio deduced from all the observations was found to be in favor of the bell with the reflector nearly as 128 to 100; and this proportion was found to be about the same for the combined observations which gave a mean average over an angle of 115°.

It will be necessary to have a much heavier bell to transmit a louder sound in the desired direction than by a reflector; thus, the economical value of that apparatus is incontestable. However, its application is restricted on account of the few places at which it could be generally placed—upon the ends of piers and on the galleries of light-houses.

DISTINCTIONS.

Special notations have been adopted in sounding the bells, so as to prevent confusion and mingling of sounds. The strokes of the bell made by simple machinery are arranged in groups, which embrace an equal number of strokes for each group, struck in regular succession, and each group is separated by intervals of greater or less duration. Thus, six, eight, or ten strokes, struck at 2 to 2, 3 to 3, or 4 to 4 seconds, followed by an interval of 15 or 20 seconds, and reproducing themselves. At the seaports, the minimum height of the water in the channel is made known by adding a simple stroke or two in the middle of the interval which separates the two succeeding groups of sounds of the bells. There is an advantage to the range of the sound in making the strokes as near together as possible, provided each one is heard distinctly; but there is an inconvenience in this on account of the necessity for more frequently winding up the machinery thus required to do more work.

The number of strokes upon the bell being much more easily noted than the elapsed time between the intervals, it is the former which is taken as the characteristic distinction, and it is readily seen that this system of distinctions is susceptible of still greater diversity than our illuminating apparatus.

CHAPTER III. STATE OF THE BEACONAGE AND BUOYAGE OF THE COASTS OF FRANCE to January 1, 1864, is omitted in the translation of this memoir.

DOCUMENTS.

I. The report containing the exposition of the system adopted by the "Commission des Phares"* to light the coasts of France, presented at its sitting, May 20, 1825, by Rear Admiral De Rossel, is omitted in this translation.

---

* The "Commission des Phares" was established by Count Molé, Director General of Bridges and Roads, April 29, 1811. It was composed at that time of—

Messrs. FERREGEAU, SGANZIN, } Inspectors General of Bridges and Roads.
TARBÉ DE VAUXCLAIRS, Divisional Inspector of Bridges and Roads.
CHARLES, MALUS, SANÉ, } Members of the Academy of Sciences.
MONTCABRIEY, JACOB, DUPERREY, } Superior Officers of the Navy.

The following have been called upon to take part successively to fill vacancies caused by deaths and resignations in the "Commission des Phares:"

Messrs. ARAGO, Member of the Institute, 1813–1853.
DE ROSSEL, Captain of line-of-battle ship, 1817–1829.
ROLLAND, Inspector General of Naval Engineering, 1817–1838.
MATHIEU, Member of the Institute, 1819.
COCHIN, Inspector General of Bridges and Roads, 1819–1825.
HALGAN, Captain of line-of-battle ship, afterwards Vice-Admiral, 1819–1834, and 1836–1849.
AUGUSTIN FRESNEL, Engineer of Bridges and Roads, Secretary to the Commission, 1824–1827.
BARON DE PRONY, Inspector General of Bridges and Roads, 1825–1839.
BEAUTEMPS BEAUPRÉ, Member of the Institute, Hydrographer in Chief of the Navy, 1826–1854.
LÉONOR FRESNEL, Engineer of Bridges and Roads, Secretary of the "Commission des Phares," and subsequently Divisional Inspector, 1827.

II. MEMOIR UPON A NEW SYSTEM OF ILLUMINATING LIGHT-HOUSES, BY A. FRESNEL, read before the members of the Academy of Sciences, July 29, 1822, has been omitted in this translation.

III. CALCULATION OF THE ELEMENTS OF LENTICULAR APPARATUS, BY M. E. ALLARD, Chief Engineer of Bridges and Roads, omitted in this translation.

IV. LIST OF PRICES OF ILLUMINATING APPARATUS AND LANTERNS, omitted.

V. DETAILED ESTIMATE OF THE ANNUAL EXPENSES OF THE ILLUMINATING SERVICE, to January 1, 1864, omitted.

VI. CONDITIONS RELATIVE TO THE SUPPLYING OF COLZA OIL, FOR THE LIGHT-HOUSE SERVICE, FOR THE COASTS OF FRANCE, omitted.

VII, VIII, IX, X. INSTRUCTIONS UPON THE SERVICE OF LENS-LIGHT APPARATUS, BEACON-LIGHTS, AND LIGHT-VESSELS, AND REGULATIONS FOR THE KEEPERS OF LIGHT-HOUSES AND BEACONS ON THE COASTS OF FRANCE, &c., have been omitted.

Messrs. LAMBLARDIE, Divisional Inspector of Bridges and Roads, Adjunct Inspector General of Naval Hydraulic Works, 1830–1841.
BARON HAMELIN, Rear Admiral, 1834–1839.
BARON DE BOUGAINVILLE, Captain of line-of-battle ship, subsequently Rear Admiral, 1834–1838, and 1841–1847.
BOUCHER, Inspector General of Naval Engineering, 1838–1851.
CASY, Captain of line-of-battle ship, 1838–1839.
MASSIEU DE CLERVAL, Rear Admiral, 1839–1841.
LE PRÉDOUR, Captain of line-of-battle ship, 1839–1847.
BERNARD, Inspector General of Bridges and Roads, and Naval Hydraulic Works, 1841–1847.
RAFFENEAU DE LISLE, Inspector General of Bridges and Roads, 1843–1846.
L. REYNAUD, Chief Engineer of Bridges and Roads, Secretary of the "Commission des Phares," and subsequently Inspector General, 1846.
DE HELL, Rear Admiral, 1847–1856.
TROTTÉ DE LA ROCHE, Inspector General of Bridges and Roads, and Naval Hydraulic Works, 1847–1857.
DE SUIN, Captain of line-of-battle ship, 1847–1849.
HAMELIN, Vice Admiral, 1849–1852.
MATHIEU, Rear Admiral, 1849.
LE BARBIER DE TINAN, Rear Admiral, 1852–1854.
LEROUX, Inspector General of Naval Engineering, 1852–1854.
DE GOURDON, Rear Admiral, 1854–1856.
GARNIER, Inspector General of Naval Engineering, 1854–1858.
BÉGAT, Chief Hydrographic Engineer of the Navy, 1854.
DUPERREY, Member of the Academy of Sciences, 1854.
JURIEN DE LA GRAVIÈRE, Rear Admiral, 1856–1858, and 1860–1861.
CHOPART, Captain of line-of-battle ship, 1856–1858.
REIBELL, Inspector General of Bridges and Roads, and Naval Hydraulic Works, 1857.
PENAUD, Rear Admiral, 1858–1859.
DUPOUY, Captain of line-of-battle ship, 1858–1859.
PRÉTOT, Inspector General of Naval Engineering, 1858.
JANNIN, Captain of line-of-battle ship, 1859–1863.
POUQUES D'HERBINGHEM, Rear Admiral, 1861–1863.
PARIS, Rear Admiral, 1863.
LABROUSSE, Rear Admiral, 1863.

INDEX.

A.

B.

C.

D.

E.

F.

G.

H.

I.

L.

M.

www.ingramcontent.com/pod-product-compliance
Lightning Source LLC
LaVergne TN
LVHW021411110826
845150LV00007B/1881

* 9 7 8 1 4 2 5 5 1 1 0 1 2 *